OVERSEAS AND UNDERSOLD

GOING GLOBAL

OVERSEAS AND UNDERSOLD

GOING GLOBAL

Australian Business Successes in the International Marketplace

David White

In association with
the Australian Trade Commission and
the Commonwealth Bank

an
ABC
BOOK

Published by ABC Enterprises in association
with the Australian Trade Commission for the
AUSTRALIAN BROADCASTING CORPORATION
20 Atchison Street (Box 4444) Crows Nest NSW 2065

National Library of Australia
Cataloguing-in-Publication entry

White, David, 1940-   .
    Going global: overseas and undersold.

    ISBN 0 7333 0024 3.

    1. Export marketing—Management—Australia. 2. Business enterprises—
    Australia. I. Australian Trade Commission. II. Commonwealth Banking
    Corporation (Australia). III. Title. IV. Title: Going global: overseas and
    undersold (Television program).

658.8480994

Set in 11pt Baskerville by Midland Typesetters, Vic
Printed and bound in Australia by Pirie Printers, Fyshwick, ACT
4.1499

Contents

Contents

Foreword

Those of us concerned with international business — and AUSTRADE is intimately involved in a wide spectrum of activities from export counselling to investment insurance — often tend to focus on issues such as the quality of market intelligence, business planning, and other strategies implicit in international marketing. International business, to say the least, involves a highly technical set of disciplines.

In the end, however, the distinction between success and failure depends on people. Good organisations devote an exceptional amount of attention to people. Good organisations are almost always headed by managers who are passionately involved in what they are doing and who can convey their vision to others.

Business, in Australia, does not adequately command the imagination of the public. Our current external debt problems are usually seen through the prism of aggregate figures, through the abstractions of large numbers, and in the context of economic policy options. Yet a path out of these problems and towards a more secure economic future requires a more internationally competitive business sector. That comes down to individual firms and to individual managers. We should never lose sight of this.

Business is never dull and it is difficult to think of any sort of business which is more exciting than that of the international scene. The challenges are more complex and therefore more interesting and potentially more rewarding. The locales vary from boardroom Tokyo to redeveloping Vietnam. The business techniques vary from Just in Time inventory to barter trade packages.

These challenges attract a rich and widely varied mix of people. David White's book, based on research material gathered for AUSTRADE'S successful *Going Global* television series, does not seek to be a text on international marketing. Instead, it illuminates the character and views of some of the successful people on the Australian side of international business. This is a valuable contribution and we can learn from these examples. It is clear that we can benefit from more people, more managers and entrepreneurs like these. Apart from appreciating the techniques which they employ, we must also recognise their passion for their businesses and their commitment to success.

The messages in this book are clear. We need to think of ourselves as part of the international business community. We must study our competitors, learn about diverse business cultures and market requirements, and create and adapt our products and services in response to the particular needs of customers in each market.

Management, the unions and the workforce as a whole must continue their joint struggle to stimulate Australian industry into one of the most efficient manufacturing sectors in the world.

Australia's economic future depends on our ability as a nation to respond to the challenges of international competition. The stories contained in this book will help to make all of us more aware of those challenges and to make us realise that we can respond to them, positively and profitably.

LINDSAY MACALISTER
Managing Director
Australian Trade Commission

Acknowledgments

Overseas and Undersold: Going Global is based on a documentary series of the same name produced by David Flatman Productions for the Australian Broadcasting Corporation in association with AUSTRADE, the Commonwealth Bank and the Australian Film Finance Corporation.

David White, the author of this book, wrote the series. But, as several crews were deployed to film in thirteen countries, no single person could have conducted all the interviews and collected all the information needed for both the series and the book. Much material was gathered by the producer, David Flatman, and directors Richard Jemison, Jim Downes and John Hosking. Editorial assistance was provided by David Flatman; David Faulks and John Hemphill of AUSTRADE; and Jan Bradley of ABC Enterprises.

Special thanks must be given to the many people who gave generously of their time and energy to enable us to relate their experiences of 'going global'. This book is their story.

1 The Challenge

As Australia enters the 1990s, there is a growing awareness that its economy has serious problems. Things have changed since Donald Horne wrote in *The Lucky Country* in 1964: 'A nation more concerned with styles of life than with achievement has managed to achieve what may be the most evenly prosperous society in the world.' In the last few years, many Australians have learned that the acquisition of wealth can require considerable effort; and that, where there is less wealth, there can be greater pressure not to share it.

It is not surprising that it took so long to learn these lessons. Australia has always had abundant natural resources with which it could pay its bills. For decades, we lived off agricultural exports; 'riding on the sheep's back' we called it. Then, in more recent times, we bought ourselves a new burst of apparent prosperity by digging up and selling minerals.

The mineral boom inspired among many Australians a pursuit of easy pickings. A sadly distinctive feature of—or substitute for—our intellectual life at the close of the 1960s was a sudden, middle-class obsession with speculation in shares and property. Many did well out of it and, downtown, the long lunch became as much a part of our culture as inefficient work practices had become in our factories.

We were breeding new heroes, too. The financial pages began to be dominated by men (there were almost no women) who made their names and their fortunes out of company takeovers and sharemarket raids. We even invented a new word—'greenmail'—to describe how some of them could extract a large profit out of cornering a vital parcel of shares; but, instead of the word denoting anything sordid, it came to symbolise cleverness. On top of all this, Australia, along with other Western countries, experienced the frenzy of a bull market which ran through the mid-1980s.

As in our past, it all seemed so easy. We ignored the fact that some of our new heroes were not building anything productive or manufacturing or growing anything substantial. Instead, they were constructing paper castles and their building materials were share scrip and loan agreements.

Therein lies an important development: increasingly, those loan agreements were being written overseas. Whereas foreign borrowing was once a matter for governments, deregulation of our financial markets in the 1980s has seen private external borrowing grow dramatically. The point has been reached where more than three-quarters of Australia's net foreign debt is private.

It would be unfair to suggest that the paper heroes were solely responsible for the increase. Much of the private overseas borrowing has been to finance imports, including capital equipment. Here the borrowing has been part of a vicious circle: we have needed more money to buy components and equipment so that we could produce more to make more money to pay off our increasing debt.

Whatever the reasons—and currency devaluations and the residual effect of heavy governmental borrowings in the early 1980s have contributed—Australia is experiencing massive indebtedness. Between 1980 and mid-1989, our gross foreign debt increased tenfold and reached $130 billion. That's $7700 for every man, woman and child.

There is currently some argument in academic circles about whether we should worry about the size of the debt. But the commonest view is that it does matter. For one thing, it affects interest rates and, in a home-owning nation, that hits a lot of people. The debt is also expensive to service—with a 1989–90 cost of about $12 billion, according to an early estimate by Paul McCarthy, the Chief Economist for the Commonwealth Bank.

'We are in trouble with not only the amount of debt we

have at the present time but the rate at which it is increasing,' John Ralph, Managing Director and Chief Executive of mining giant, CRA Ltd, warned in mid-1989, 'and consequently we can't go on as we are today because we will get to a level of debt where other people will not want to lend money to us to pay for the level of consumption that we're currently enjoying.'

To stabilise its debt, Australia, among other things, needs to boost its exports and rein in its imports. At present, they are very much out of balance: in 1988–89 our current account deficit—which, in broad terms, measures that balance—was worsening at the rate of close to $2 million every hour of every day.

The Economic Planning Advisory Council (EPAC), which represents government, industry, unions and community groups, estimated in mid-1989 that debt stabilisation required a current account deficit of around 2.5 per cent of Gross Domestic Product (GDP). In fact, EPAC noted, 'the current account deficit is running at about 4.5–5.5 per cent of GDP'. As recently as 1979–80, it was only 1.7 per cent.

'It's a very serious problem,' Senator John Button, the Minister in the Hawke Government responsible for Australia's export drive, said in June 1989. 'Australia in the last few decades has become a relatively rich country by exporting raw materials. Now raw materials are not going to be as significant in the world trading situation in the future as they have been in the past and we have to diversify our economy into a wider range of exports. Otherwise, with the decline in commodities around the world, this country will gradually lose income and that will affect the standard of living of every Australian.'

Laurie Carmichael, Assistant Secretary of the ACTU, says that the living standards of some Australians have already fallen and he describes the current situation as 'frightening'. Living standards are really at stake in this country but it needs to be understood it's not a short-term thing,' he says.

Carmichael has emerged as an especially interesting figure in this discussion. A leader of the Amalgamated Metal Workers Union for many years, he was the quintessential radical ogre to Australian business and the Right generally. Now, from his ACTU position, he is being seen in a quite different light. This is because of the major role he has taken in encouraging the restructuring of Australian industry to make it more competitive. It is not that he has suddenly gone soft on his old opponents: he describes what he and other union leaders are doing as 'filling in for the abysmal performance of Australian management'.

In 1986, Carmichael was a member of a mission jointly sent by the ACTU and the Trade Development Council to examine the economies and industrial structures of Western Europe. Its report, published under the title *Australia Reconstructed*, is a seminal document in signalling the trend in the trade-union movement to seek the kind of industrial changes which would boost the country's exports. Its exposition of some of the country's basic problems remains very pertinent:

> *Ours is a middle-sized economy which is largely unable to influence international economic conditions, yet is largely subject to them. For a considerable period, the prices received for our exports have not kept pace with increases paid for our imports. . . On top of this, Australia's export composition, which is weighted towards low value-added agricultural and mineral products, runs against the trend in world trade towards sophisticated manufactures and services. In addition, our agricultural exports are increasingly encountering trade barriers and facing severe price competition from subsidised agricultural products in world markets, while many of our mineral exports are also subject to increased competition, coincident with slower growth in demand.*

The diagnosis points to a cure: Australia must markedly increase its exports of manufactured goods and services. But, to do that, we have to overcome some deep-seated problems.

In 1984–85, manufactures accounted for only 16.9 per cent of Australia's merchandise exports—that is, exports of goods but not services. By 1987–88—after several years of strong promotion by the Federal Government through such bodies as the Australian Trade Commission (AUSTRADE) and the Department of Industry, Technology and Commerce (DITAC)—this had risen to 21.2 per cent. This has occurred largely at the expense of mineral exports. But mineral and farm produce exports still far outweigh manufactures. Minerals accounted for 37.7 per cent of exports of goods in 1987–88 (down 6.3 per cent from 1984–85) and farm produce for 38.7 per cent (up slightly), a total of 76.4 per cent of our merchandise exports.

There are other indicators of improvement with manufactures. Exports of what the statisticians call 'simply transformed manufactures' (STMs)—such things as unworked iron and steel and chemicals—rose by 37.4 per cent from 1986–87 to 1987–88. Exports of 'elaborately transformed manufactures' (ETMs), which include computers, cars, footwear and so on, rose by 19 per cent in the same period.

DITAC's 1987–88 annual report pointed out that Australia had joined the list of the top ten countries supplying processed and manufactured goods to the Japanese market. 'Australia now out-performs Canada, Singapore and Hong Kong in the Japanese market for value added products,' the report noted. 'Exports [to Japan] of ETMs alone, including automotive components, scientific instruments and machinery reached $212 million in 1987, a rise of 35 per cent over 1986.'

But, with a drollness uncharacteristic of such official documents, DITAC's report warned against too much optimism: 'Although some commentators are now speaking of a renaissance in manufacturing industry, it is perhaps truer, though less exciting to say that the manufacturing sclerosis which had looked like a terminal condition in the early 1980s is well on the way to being healed.'

How did the patient become so sick? Paul McCarthy, of the Commonwealth Bank, has no doubt: 'In my view, the underlying reason is, in fact, the protectionist environment under which our manufacturing sector grew up in the post-war period. It fostered an inward-looking manufacturing sector . . . While the world economy was growing rapidly and while there was strong demand for our primary products, then we could go on ignoring the problem. But the chickens have really come home to roost in the latter part of the 1980s.'

Protectionism has, in fact, both encouraged a variety of ills and interacted with others. EPAC, in a paper entitled *Australia's Medium Term Growth Potential* (March 1988), gives this assessment:

> *A major problem is that some Australian industries have not been able to take advantage of scale economies. This partly reflects our distance from foreign markets and internal geography. But it has also been aggravated by 'inward-looking', and unco-ordinated industry policies (at both Federal and State levels) during much of the post-war period, as well as inefficiencies in the domestic transport system.*
>
> *There has also been an associated tendency towards inefficient work practices and a bias, on the part of both labour and management, against skill-acquisition and innovation. In consequence we have arguably been slow in applying new technologies and in identifying and correcting inefficiencies.*

Protectionism ensured domestic markets for our manufactures and thus discouraged all but the adventurous from selling overseas. When we did go overseas, we tended to rely on our ties with the likes of Britain and the United States. If there is a word which sums up the dominant characteristic of the protectionist era, it is 'comfort'.

Senator John Button agrees: 'Have we been too comfortable? I think my answer to that is yes. The countries which have done best in world trade are the countries which have to do it to survive. Look at Japan—no resources, yet a miracle performer in economic terms because they've had to do it. And you get other countries . . . small countries like the Netherlands, who have been great trading nations for a very long time; they export almost double from the same size population that Australia exports. They see the world as their market and they go after it. We've got to do that.'

So how great are the opportunities for our manufactured goods and services? In a December 1988 publication, *International Business Opportunities*, AUSTRADE compared the actual export performance of industry groups in 1986-87 with 'possible targets' based on market opportunities, in 1991-92. It projected higher annual growth rates for manufactures and services than for any of the other groups—food, materials and energy.

It said that over the five-year period, exports of manufactured goods could grow in value from $10.29 billion to $19.65 billion—an annual growth rate of 13.8 per cent. Within this group, it foresaw simply transformed manufactures rising annually by 11.5 per cent to $9.22 billion and elaborately transformed manufactures by 16.1 per cent to $10.42 billion.

For services, it suggested that exports could grow in value from $6.8 billion to $12.19 billion, an annual rate of 12.4 per cent. In this group, tourism would be the biggest winner, rising from $3.42 billion to $7.58 billion, or 17.3 per cent a year. (That last estimate, however, was before Australia's airline pilots pricked the tourism balloon with their 1989 strike.)

Manufactures and services would combine to account for 48.7 per cent of all export earnings in 1991–92, compared to only 40.2 per cent in 1986–87. The improvement becomes even more interesting if processed foods, which involve value-added transformation, are tallied up with manufactures and services. Together, the three groups could account for 54.1 per cent of all exports. Unusually for Australia, this would mean unprocessed food, other rural materials, minerals and energy becoming minority contributors to our trade balance—falling from 56.3 per cent to 45.9 per cent.

In a February 1989 publication, *Strategic Directions*, AUSTRADE said it expected North Asia, especially Japan, to be the major growth market for both simply transformed manufactures and processed foods. New Zealand was expected to be the major growing market for elaborately transformed manufactures; other significant and growing markets would be the United States, Japan, Germany, the UK, Hong Kong, India, Korea, China and Taiwan. While the growth in foreign earnings from services is likely to be dominated by tourism, other important areas are computer software, where the markets are worldwide, and education where the biggest markets are likely to be in Asia.

All of AUSTRADE'S projections involve 'market-driven assessments'. 'The reality remains that the capturing of these opportunities will require determined efforts by Australia to overcome various constraints,' it warns in *International Business Opportunities*.

One major constraint is the recent trend towards the creation of new and powerful trading blocs. These might put fresh barriers in the path of international trade. Australia, along with other countries, awaits with some anxiety the trade unification of the European Economic Community in 1992; there is concern that this might lead to a closed European market. A free trade agreement between the United States and Canada means a further integration of the North American market. And Japan is already a one-nation colossus with a trading system which inhibits penetration by many foreign goods.

There is already conflict between Europe and the US over agricultural trade and between Japan and the US over manufactured goods. If these tensions are resolved by deals between these three dominant trading groups, it might well be that Australia and other small nations are left out in the cold.

Australia also faces interesting challenges from newly industrialising countries, such as Korea and Taiwan. In *Australia's Medium Term Growth Potential*, EPAC predicts that their growth will generally work to Australia's advantage because their economies will provide potential markets for our products. But it warns: 'Their increasing share of manufactures trade will constrain Australia's ability to radically lift its own export performance in this area.' It will be an important test to see whether the opportunities outweigh the increased competition.

Not all of the constraints are external. New products for the world market are essential but Australia has a low level of commitment to research and development in industry. Up to 1985, private sector R & D spending was only 0.2 per cent of Gross Domestic Product, compared with a median level for comparable OECD countries of around one per cent. In May 1985, the Federal Government introduced special tax incentives for R & D and these have boosted spending in this area quite dramatically—by 25 per cent in the first year and 20 per cent in the second. But, because the figures are rising from such a small base, private sector investment in R & D still represents only 0.42 per cent of GDP.

This is one example of an area in which Australian industry and business leaders have to change their attitudes. Above all, we have to develop a new and aggressive orientation to export—an 'export culture' some call it—if we are to reverse our declining trading performance.

There are Australians who are already tackling these problems. They are not typical. Otherwise, the problems would not exist. But their activities—and their energy, commitment and skills—might provide leads for others to follow. So, having described the broad trading situation confronting us, the rest of this book tells what some of them are doing. Anecdotally, it describes their products, their marketing methods, their management styles. It shows what efforts are being made to change the Australian workplace and our most troubled transport link—the waterfront—so that we can become more export-competitive. Finally, it describes the experiences of some newcomers to international trade.

If we need heroes on the financial pages of our newspapers, better it be some of the people who are making and selling products which the rest of the world values than the builders of paper castles.

2 The Products

THE biggest single export from Port Botany in Sydney, which has Australia's newest and most efficient container facilities, is empty space. Each month, 160 000 containers arrive there full of imported cargo. More than 50 000 are returned with nothing in them. The void in those containers symbolises our need to boost our exports of value-added products, especially manufactures.

How do we find the products to fill the containers? In trying to provide some clues to the mystery, this book's main concern is with the so-called 'elaborately transformed manufactures' (ETMs). It looks at people and products in this area, although it also touches on examples from other fields of activity, such as services, minerals and metals.

AUSTRADE has identified four broad areas of opportunity for Australian goods in the ETM category. High technology is one of them. Here Australia has particularly good prospects with biotechnology, medical and scientific equipment and avionics and some other aerospace activities.

A second area is the leisure industry. In these troubled times, it is ironic that the Australian passion for sport and other leisure activities can be a blessing, as well as a curse. The blessing is that we can make things ranging from fashion clothing to sporting equipment (which encompasses a very wide territory—right up to yachts and motor cruisers).

A third area involves a potentially large and varied range of products: helping provide the physical infrastucture in developing countries, particular in Asia. Their infrastuctural needs include ports, railways, other transport facilities, power generation and telecommunications.

A fourth possibility lies in the intensification of what AUSTRADE terms 'intra-industry trade' and its extension to North and South-East Asian countries. In its publication, *International Business Opportunities*, AUSTRADE says: 'An example of intra-industry trade is in the automotive industry where Australia's expanding trade in vehicles and parts is largely due to the international sourcing arrangements of companies operating in many markets. As the Asian countries, especially the NICs [newly industrialised countries], expand their industrial base, there should be increasing opportunities for Australia to work with those countries in integrating their manufacturing operations.'

But these are not the only opportunities for Australian manufactured goods. If a product and the people behind it are good enough—in every sense, from preparation to back-up service—markets can open up in surprising places. And the opportunities are not restricted simply to large organisations with big factories and representatives scattered around the world. This chapter looks at the success which has been won by a collection of small, medium and big operators. Their products are in three fields nominated by AUSTRADE—high technology, transport and fashion clothing—but not necessarily in the predicted places.

Electro Optic Systems Pty Ltd is a small company operating from almost laughably modest premises outside Canberra. But, in three years, it has established itself in the highest of high technology. When the United States launches a giant orbiting space platform in 1995, it will carry laser equipment designed by EOS. The company shows that high-tech offers unlimited scope for those with the scientific, industrial and marketing know-how.

But there are opportunities in more traditional, mainstream areas. The McKay group of Melbourne has produced agricultural implements for nearly 60 years. But now it is chalking up impressive export results with a very different product: a clip for fastening railway lines to concrete sleepers. With it, McKay is helping to transform the railroads of North America.

While the McKay group is attacking a high-volume market with a simple low-cost product, Brisbane designer Anne

Lewin is appealing to an altogether different American and Asian audience with something much more exotic—expensive lingerie.

Finally, this chapter shows that you do not have to make something so tangible to be successful in world markets. TNT, one of Australia's corporate giants, sells a product that you cannot feel, taste or smell. What TNT delivers is service—the service of moving freight quickly. It is so good at it that, in terms of the size of its network and its range of services, it now claims to be the world's biggest transport organisation. Of special interest is what it is currently doing in Europe. It has recently snared leadership of the express airfreight market in Western Europe and, at the same time, has moved decisively into the Eastern bloc.

While TNT's success is extraordinary, it is the very ordinariness of its product that gives its Chief Executive, Sir Peter Abeles, hope for the capacity of Australian business leaders to change their thinking about export with enough speed to turn around Australia's trading position: 'My colleagues and I, in our own little world, have changed fast enough and, therefore, if it can be done by just a carrier, which is not a very special profession—if it can be done by just a carrier, there are many others who could speed up this process and I hope they will.'

High-tech conjures up images of modern offices, laboratories and production facilities; of companies housed in buildings and 'technology parks' designed to match the contemporaneity of their products. Not so for Dr Ben Greene and his Electro Optic Systems Pty Ltd. His premises are one level of a modest two-storey building in Queanbeyan, on the outskirts of Canberra. Incongruously, they sit above a greengrocer's shop—Freddie Frapples Fruit Shop, to give it its full, alliterative name.

'The location was chosen quite deliberately so that we could be out of the public eye,' Greene, who is Managing Director of EOS, says, 'and we had a task we'd set ourselves and we wanted to just have peace and quiet and a location where we could get on with it. We didn't need a shopfront in this country because we don't do business here.'

EOS does business elsewhere at the very leading edge of high technology—laser systems. Although fully operational only since 1986, it is already engaged in work ranging from satellite communications in Saudi Arabia to the preparation of laser equipment for the US space-platform launching in 1995.

Its premises reflect an impatient, 'do-or-die' approach which characterised its beginnings. 'Initially, we wanted to make or break and do that as quickly as possible,' Greene says. 'So we targeted what we thought were the three toughest markets and, at the same time, the three most prestigious markets. That's Japan, West Germany and the United States. And we figured that, if we could break into those markets, we would be able to break into any market in the world and we have been very successful.' He is not a shrinking violet in assessing that success: 'I thought it would take a little longer than it has. We've effectively dominated and we've monopolised the market areas that we targeted initially.'

The speciality of EOS is laser ranging technology and its applications. That means being able to do such things as pinpoint the position of objects in space with an accuracy of half a millimetre. That capacity for precise measurement is one of the attributes it will bring to the US space-station program.

The company has in its early years focused on contracts of a certain size—ones modest enough to have limited appeal to major high-tech companies but too big for smaller, undercapitalised companies. That translates into sharing in projects worth between $10 million and $100 million. At the top end of that scale, such as the US space platform, it will seek a big partner with whom to make a joint bid. At the lower end, it will control the projects but farm out some specialised work. Over a period of more than two years to mid-1989, EOS was involved in projects worth around $100 million; its share was about $5 million.

A good example of how it can share work is its Saudi Arabian deal. The contract, won in 1988, involves building a mobile satellite communication system mounted on a trailer, comprising a 75 cm telescope, a laser generator and a transmit/receive optical system, combined with a computerised timing system. From experience, Greene and his colleagues know that the Contraves Goerz Corporation, a US-based multinational, is in the forefront of optical systems. Under Ronald Reagan's presidency, it became involved, for example, in developmental work for what he called the 'strategic defense initiative' and which others termed 'Star Wars'. So, EOS has ordered $1.3 million worth of optical equipment from Contraves for the Saudi project.

Greene explains the contribution EOS can make to projects of this kind: 'Our product is really technological know-how, generically speaking. We can walk into a wide range of high-technology project situations where the client requires a solution to a particular problem . . . and . . . we can put up a high-technology solution to that—which might be a space-borne system—and we can prove in advance of the product that the product will work. In other words, it's a matter of designing a prototyping facility to prove to a client that we have a solution and we will deliver it and this is how much it will cost.'

That means that EOS has not established significant manufacturing facilities either in Australia or overseas. Greene believes that gives the company an advantage in competing for contracts: 'For every hundred dollars that we sell into a market, we will offset about 80 per cent directly back into the domestic industries of that country and, by not having fixed manufacturing facilities in any particular offshore location, we can cut every deal tailor-made to the government that we are dealing with. So, whichever government it is, we can say to them, "We will locate this amount of work into your country, based upon us slicing out the parts that really can't possibly be done here and the rest of it will be done here".'

This approach has enabled EOS to operate with a very small workforce. And the composition of that workforce explains how the company could move so quickly into international high technology deals. It consists of only a dozen people, most of whom have worked together for up to 15 years, first as Federal Government scientists before they decided to pit their skills against the best in the world of high-tech commerce. This is clearly a place for high achievers and none personifies that better than Greene.

After graduating from the University of Queensland with an honours degree in electrical engineering, he joined the Department of Defence as an experimental officer in 1972. His work in lasers goes back to that period. In 1974, he switched to the Department of Resources and Energy, where he stayed until he left to set up EOS. While employed there he gained a Doctor of Philosophy from the University of Hull in England.

His curriculum vitae for his last five years with Resources and Energy points very clearly in the direction of his EOS activities. Under a contract with the US National Aeronautics and Space Administration (NASA), he was responsible for developing new technology laser systems. He negotiated bilateral and multilateral international agreements and administered international projects. He directed the Orroral Geodetic Observatory, near Canberra, which contains enormously powerful laser ranging equipment developed as part of the NASA satellite tracking system; Greene and some of his EOS colleagues were the ones who developed it.

Thus the technological capabilities which the group has packaged under the EOS banner were already well advanced before being launched into the commercial market. And so were the contacts needed in that market, and the knowledge of how it works. This was one company which did not need to spend a couple of years developing its product and marketing techniques in the domestic market and then carry out a painstaking export survey. Its feet were running the moment EOS hit the ground. Greene sums up their advantages: 'We knew that there were niches and we knew that there were market requirements that weren't being properly met and we also knew we had the technology and the organisational capabilities to go in there and compete and win and, beyond that, be successful—deliver a good quality product.'

Proving itself internationally before worrying about the domestic market is 'not a formula I recommend to any company,' Greene says. 'We had a very, very good corporate plan, we had the right kind of backing fiscally and we had extremely good marketing arrangements in place very early in our company's history.'

EOS has also received substantial input from AUSTRADE. All of its contracts so far have been implemented through AUSTRADE's International Projects Division. The division is able to act on a government-to-government level with foreign official agencies and provide them with financial and performance guarantees. Greene acknowledges that, in its dealings on his behalf, AUSTRADE has 'demonstrated the practical assistance available to small Australian companies when dealing with large overseas clients, particularly government agencies'.

The scientific background of its key personnel ensures that EOS has a substantial research and development program which, in the tough-guy language that Greene sometimes uses, 'delivers us weapons that we can use in the marketing war'. There is also 'a management philosophy that will back a technologist when he says, "I can do it— I can deliver that particular feature and this is how much it will cost".'

With EOS, technology and marketing are constantly intertwined. A touch of the tough guy appears again: 'A typical project will cost us in marketing expenses alone up to half a million dollars, and we can't afford to go into that sort of situation half-hearted and we take no prisoners. It's literally trench warfare and we've never lost—we've never lost a bid.' Why not? 'In conventional marketing terms because our product is better specified, better quality and more competitively priced than anyone else's but, in practical terms, it's because, whenever the situation arises where we're in tight competitive situations, we draw on technology. That's always our ace in the hole.'

He explains how that 'ace in the hole' is played: 'In situations where we have one product against another product and we have a competitor who looks like a realistic competitor, then we go beyond what the client says he wants and we find out what, deep in the recesses of his subconscious, he would really like and we explore the wish list. And we find invariably that we have the technology to deliver a larg proportion of that, and those are cards that we usually play downstream in the negotiating process, where we will table certain technological features that other companies say can't be done.'

The most important contract won by EOS so far is to participate in the development of a geoscience laser ranging system (GLRS) for NASA for inclusion in the space-platform project. To compete for it, EOS directed a substantial amount of its internal R & D towards the specific problems which could be expected for laser radars in the space environment. Then, in 1988, it went into a project team with the McDonnell Douglas Electronic Systems Company (MDESC), part of a huge US aerospace conglomerate, which is the prime contractor to NASA for the GLRS project.

Why did MDESC bring EOS into the team? 'Their technology is the best that's available and that's why,' responds Jimmy D. McGrew, laser communications systems integration engineer for the US company. 'We go where the best system is—whether it's locally or down-under.' Greene is proud of his involvement: 'We believe this is one of the most prestigious high-technology contracts ever won by Australian industry since it involves the ground-up design and development of a sophisticated space-borne system against open international competition.' It will also be financially worthwhile: the GLRS technology will ultimately involve NASA expenditure of more than $US100 million and EOS aims to get a significant proportion of that.

The GLRS will be, in Greene's words, 'the first planetary sensor capable of making global measurements of the early characteristics of the predicted greenhouse cycle'. By aiming laser beams from the space platform at the earth's surface, the system will monitor changes in global sea levels, polar ice caps and cloud formations. The project, he says, 'really is bordering on an altruistic project'. 'One trains to be a scientist and one always hopes that one can be of use to mankind. That's the goal and it's seldom reached in career paths.'

Not that all of his work can bring this kind of warm, inner glow. Clearly, laser technology has military uses. EOS is already carrying out experimental work with MDESC with the aim of incorporating laser sensors in McDonnell Douglas fighter planes. And, in Pittsburgh on a visit to Contraves Goerz, Greene jumps aboard a rotating mount to test a high-speed tracking system which can locate, measure and film airborne and ground-based military and intelligence targets. He sees the potential for integration of EOS laser systems with this technology.

High technology does not define the limits of Greene's ambition. He is looking for another company—bigger than EOS and with a product range reaching into lower technology—to take over. 'We plan to use EOS as an image-making vehicle for a larger corporate structure, which will come underneath [EOS and] which needn't necessarily be involved in high technology products,' he says. He is necessarily coy about specifics but says: 'We do have a prejudice towards the aerospace industry and we have a very strong technology in lasers, computer systems, software systems development and micro-electronics—micro-micro-electronics.' The target company would be involved broadly in such areas.

With this move, EOS will acquire a proper manufacturing base for the first time. The rooms above Freddie Frapples Fruit Shop won't be big enough anymore.

The Melbourne-based McKay group is almost the opposite of EOS. The young Queanbeyan company has been able to achieve some good financial results quickly on the basis of a market-wise display of scientific pyrotechnics; by Australian standards, McKay is a long-established company with a record of patient commitment to relatively low-technology, high-volume industrial products.

But the contrast is not between intelligence and dullness. For McKay's biggest export success of the last decade has been based on something very clever: the railways equivalent of a better mousetrap. It has devised Safelok—a simple steel synthetic-rubber and plastic fastener which fixes rail track to sleepers. Unlike the traditional metal dog-spike which it is replacing, the device can be used with sleepers of any material but comes into its own with concrete.

In achieving export success with Safelok, McKay has shown enormous tenacity and, above all, belief in a product. The track fastener has also provided the company with an important means of diversification at a time when its traditional products, which had served it well for half a century, were in decline. Again, there is cleverness in the way in which it has converted industrial skills, gained from producing those older products, to a new use.

The company was founded in Melbourne in 1932 to manufacture agricultural implements and components. It became dominant in Australia with its agricultural discs and ground-working tools, such as plough and harrow discs, tillage sweeps and rotary hoe blades used by farmers to cultivate the soil. It went into export as early as 1935 when it shipped an order to New Zealand. But export was still only about 10 per cent of McKay's company sales by the 1960s, even though its products went to about 35 countries.

The company had been examining the possibilities of substantial expansion into North America when, in the late 1960s, Australia suffered a rural recession. The North American move made sense as a means of offsetting the inevitable downturn in domestic sales. It was a success. In fact, McKay could not satisfy North American demand for its products from Australia so it built another factory in Regina, Saskatchewan, Canada. By the mid-1970s, overseas markets were taking around half of McKay's products.

The Regina plant remains 'a nice and profitable little factory' in the words of A. P. 'Sandy' McCall, General Manager of McKay Rail Products, and the company is still an active exporter of farming implements from Australia. But recession has become part of the rural landscape in many places and the company recognised some time ago that the markets for agricultural tillage components would decline gradually. So, as early as the mid-1970s, it began looking for new fields of activity. The result has been for McKay to move into the manufacture of Safelok, truck wheels and industrial gearboxes.

With the manufacture of truck wheels, as with Safelok, the company showed a smart anticipation of market trends. Tubeless tyres came into general use on truck wheels much more slowly than they did on cars. But in 1978 McKay made the decision that their widespread adoption was only a matter of time. So it began concentrating on making wheels for tubeless tyres. With wheel factories in Sydney and Melbourne, it has now become the only truck wheel manufacturer in Australia.

Before this decision, however, it had begun to develop Safelok. A McKay director, Norman Pardoe, had become interested in the increasing use of concrete sleepers overseas, largely because of another directorship he held in Readymix Concrete. The railways of the world were—and are—undergoing a major transformation: passengers were becoming fewer but, in their place, freight loads were getting bigger and heavier. Freight cars with an individual capacity of as much as 120 tonnes were coming into use and, to use them most efficiently, they were being pulled at higher speeds. To carry the extra loads, concrete sleepers were starting to take over from timber.

Pardoe knew that the new sleepers lacked a truly efficient fastening device. There was a particular technical problem: how to fix rails to them with enough 'give' to ensure the metal–concrete join would last a long time. He pointed out to his fellow McKay directors that the company had considerable expertise in metal-bending which it might be able to apply profitably if it could solve the rail-fastening problem. In fact, given the size of the railroads of the world, the profit potential was huge.

By 1979, McKay had come up with the Safelok system. It consists of a shoulder and a clip, both made of steel, a synthetic-rubber pad and a plastic insulator. The shoulder is cast in the concrete sleeper. The two-pronged clip, which can be quickly put into position with simple hand tools, grips on to the shoulder at one end and locks down on the rail at the other. The insulator goes between the clip and the rail, and the pad underneath the rail; they combine to help give the system the elasticity which it needs for durability. McKay says that once a track is laid with Safelok it should not need 'respiking' regauging or other maintenance for the life of the sleeper.

When it surveyed the potential market for Safelok, McKay

resisted the temptation to go after installation on rapid transit lines, which were being laid in cities around the world at the time. 'We took the view that the real growth was going to come from the North American market, where the track was essentially on timber sleepers and where there was a great deal of pressure on the railroads to move to a more stable and better type of track,' Sandy McCall, a Scot with a thick brogue, says.

But it was one thing to have a good product and a target market. It was another to win market acceptance. Some railway engineers predicted that that would take 25 years, according to McCall. In the event, it took long enough— close to eight years. 'I guess the reason it took so long was the conservatism of the railway engineer,' he says.

To prove its product, McKay built test tracks, first in Australia and then in Canada and the United States. The sites chosen offered the most difficult conditions in the world. They ranged from the heat of the world's heaviest-haul railroad from the Hammersley iron-ore deposits in outback Australia to a site in Canada where the track was subjected to climatic change from 50°C below freezing to 40°C above in the course of a year; the terrain varied from desert to the steep inclines and tight curves of the Rocky Mountains.

'We never expected it to be easy getting into railways,' McCall says. 'I guess what encouraged us was the fact that we've always been reasonably good at reading markets and seeing where markets were going, particularly growth markets . . . So we just back our judgment as far as railways are concerned. Sure, there were some rough times; there were times when, around the board table, I guess we wondered where we were going with this. You know, another test track—when are we going to start getting paid? But we never backed off. We kept going and it's certainly paid off now.'

It took until 1985 before McKay got its first order: engineers for the Australian National Railways decided to use the local product on the Perth–Port Augusta track. It came at the right time because it provided a proving ground just in time for a far bigger contract in the United States.

Burlington Northern, the largest private railroad in the United States, decided to put concrete sleepers on two thousand kilometres of its 40 000 kilometres of track. The conversion involved laying 3.5 million sleepers. As each sleeper would require four Safelok fasteners, that meant a potential order of 14 million of the devices. It was to be the biggest single contract of its kind ever let. 'Naturally, everybody under the sun that was manufacturing fasteners decided to have a crack at that particular contract,' McCall says, 'and we, to some extent, were outsiders.'

To prove the superiority of its product, McKay took the Burlington North engineers on a tour of its test tracks—first in North America and then in Australia. All those years of effort paid off. In October 1986, Burlington Northern gave McKay a $US50 million contract over five years.

McKay swung a factory in Adelaide into increased production to meet the order. But the order involved more than the manufacturing process. The company had to make sure of the intallation of its system and provide service follow-up. To ensure that it did this thoroughly, it set up an office in Kansas City, Missouri, and staffed it with engineers. 'We wouldn't do any business at all with the railroads in North America without having the engineering liaison group to back us up,' McCall says. 'These blokes are working with the railway engineers defining needs. We don't just supply a clip prepared in this way or another little fastening system.

'Safelok is a total technology package to the railroads. We advise them on track equipment. We also manufacture the track equipment for installing Safelok . . . for gauging lines. We've got hand tools. We supply equipment to the major manufacturers of track installation equipment to enable them to do it. So we provide the railroads with a package of equipment and technological support. Our group of engineers in Kansas City provides that liaison between McKay and Burlington Northern or Union Pacific or Canadian Pacific [and] they are in constant communication with Adelaide. Adelaide is our technical base for the world . . . If Burlington Northern have a problem on track and come to us, we've got to have an answer for them within 24 hours at the latest and that's what we do.'

McKay sent John Piekarski from Adelaide to be part of the Kansas City group, which is run by an American, Rober

Magnuson. Piekarski sums up his role as doing 'a lot of watching, a lot of teaching and, I suppose, a lot of learning myself'. He adds: 'I think it's very important to have somebody from Australia here on the spot because we're here . . . to get everything moving immediately, instead of waiting for somebody else to find out what the problem is by sending letters backwards and forwards to Australia.'

Piekarski keeps in constant touch with the men working an extraordinary US-built machine, in which Safelok technology is incorporated, to put in concrete sleepers on Burlington Northern's track. The machine—a factory on wheels—looks like an invention for a Mad Max movie. It is pulled by a locomotive and consists of a series of carriages stretching for about 400 metres. It pulls out the dog-spikes in existing wooden sleepers, before executing its cleverest manoeuvre: it spreads the rails so that the timber sleepers can be jemmied out, picked up and stowed. Gantries run along the top of the machine to bring the new concrete sleepers into their loading position. As the timber sleepers are pulled up by the machine, the concrete ones are dumped in their place. The Safelok synthetic-rubber pads are positioned before the rail line is pushed back to the right gauge. Then the Safelok clips are put in place, ready for another machine to clamp them on. On a flat stretch, the machine might change the sleepers on 1200 metres of track in a day.

With a reputation as leaders in rail technology, Burlington Northern's use of Safelok has aroused significant interest in the fastener among other railways in North America. In 1989 McKay won a small order to install 50 000 concrete sleepers for Union Pacific. 'I don't think we're all of a sudden going to see a great gush of orders from North America,' McCall says, 'but I think it will be a gradual progression of the heavy-haul railroads moving into concrete and upgrading track and that will take place over the next ten years . . . So the potential is there and so is McKay.'

The stakes are indeed enormous. By the end of the current McKay contract, only 5 per cent of Burlington Northern's lines will be laid on concrete sleepers. The figure is less than one per cent for other North American railroads.

Something like 22 million timber sleepers are still laid every year in the United States alone. McKay aims to be around when they rip them up and replace them with concrete.

Australia has a long tradition of exporting basic commodities for others to process into something much more valuable. So it's a switch for an Australian to import fabrics from Europe and South-East Asia and transform them in a Brisbane factory into upmarket fashions for the rest of the world. In doing that, Anne Lewin demonstrates well the concept of high value-added exports. Her products also exemplify the importance of quality in overseas markets.

Her products are expensive lingerie—'under garments and lounge wear for the most discerning, aware and tasteful markets in the world,' according to one of her PR handouts. They range from bras, French knickers and garter belts to nightdresses and robes. Using elegant designs and hand-finishing, she makes them with lace from Chantilly in France and St Gallen in Switzerland; fine, sheer wools from Italy; and, above all, imported silk. 'Ms Lewin says no other cloth matches silk's extraordinary combination of physical and emotive qualities,' the handout declares.

She has been exporting to the United States since 1986, predominantly to stores on the east coast, such as Bergdorf Goodman, Barney's, Saks of 5th Avenue, Neiman Marcus, Bonwit Teller and the Nordstrom chain—in total, close to 50 outlets. She has found that they needed her as much as she needed them.

'What's happened in America over the last few years is that all of the stores have filled their departments with private label [products]; they make their own things in Hong Kong very cheaply,' she says. 'Now they've bored the customers to tears by having everything the same and they're desperate for interesting designer merchandise. But they're also not prepared to pay European prices. The prices from Europe are enormous. They're double our price.'

There was also a yawning gap in the product range: 'Most of the lingerie on this market is either from France or it's relatively poor quality domestic merchandise.' That gap has become her niche. But her own quality aims have had to remain as high as possible: 'We've always been very conscious of the fact that, if we're going to be successful in this market, we have to be good and we have to be as good or better than the French.'

Along with the quality, she emphasises strong back-up for her products: 'We've really targeted our market. We found 40 or 50 stores we want to sell to here and we've really gone after them. We try to look after them with marketing and advertising.' Part of this is constantly seeking exposure in the glossy magazines. 'If you're not in the magazines, you're nowhere in America,' she says.

It's an easy place to be nowhere in: 'It's a pretty tough market here. People don't mess about. If you make mistakes, they just forget you, that's it. You've got to deliver on time, you have to give them good merchandise, give them no trouble. That's the whole thing with America: give them no trouble because, if you give them trouble, there are 50 000 people ready to fill your boots.'

In her first year in the US market, 1986–87, her overseas sales totalled $A110 000. The next year, they reached $A500 000. By 1989–90, the target was $A1 million. This includes sales to Lane Crawford, a department store in Hong Kong, Holt Renfrew in Canada and major stores in Singapore and Japan.

She is approaching the Japanese, her newest quarry, with great care: 'The Japanese market's quite different. One good thing is that they love quality; they're fanatics about it and they won't buy anything else. In the American market, they will buy other things; they don't mind buying poor quality. They're not as educated as the Japanese . . .

'We have one customer who has five stores in different cities, so it's fairly early days for us in Japan. I'm really concentrating on looking after her and finding out about the Japanese market . . . The distribution system is very different in Japan. You don't just go over, set yourself up and start selling to them. You have to find a wholesaler who has associations with certain retailers.' To understand the system and its customers, she is researching the market through visits, discussions with others trading there and with information from AUSTRADE.

At 34, Anne Lewin now spends about eight months of the year overseas. At home, she has her manufacturing and administrative headquarters in the Brisbane suburb of Albion. There she has a staff of 40, with her mother, Wendy, as production manager. It was her mother who first gave her an interest in the clothing industry. Wendy Lewin has brought many years of skills and knowledge of garment construction to her daughter's business. She originally designed children's wear, so her daughter grew up surrounded by fabrics, sewing machines and patterns.

Anne Lewin founded her own company in 1980 after two years of working as a fashion agent. She had calculated that fine lingerie was about to undergo a renaissance so, right from the start, she designed modern garments, often made with traditional materials and trimmings, for a kind of woman at the top of the market: 'It's a woman who has good taste. She's educated. She likes good quality.'

After about five years, she decided to investigate the US market and, through a New York agent, almost immediately sold her garments to Bergdorf Goodman, Barney's, Saks of 5th Avenue and other noted retailers. The trouble was that the orders outstripped her capacity to finance them. Her Brisbane accountant—soon to be her ex-accountant—advised her to avoid expansion and stay out of export. She ignored his advice and, through her bank manager, attracted a $500 000, 25 per cent equity investment in her company from Business Loans and Equity Capital Limited, a group associated with Westpac.

The money enabled the firm to fill those first US orders and then go on to establish its own offices and showroom on three floors of a fashionable New York brownstone. She spends a lot of her time there now, as she insists on staying involved with retail buyers. She also travels frequently to Europe to visit quality fabric houses. Wherever she goes she takes a notebook with her to jot down ideas for designs for her constantly changing collection. In the US, she releases at least five new ranges a year. 'I love change and that's one of the reasons the collections are always so successful. People copy us, but they're always too late. We've moved on.'

She has never had any truck with gimmicks—including flavour-of-the-month Australianness. She sees no role for that in her product area: 'There's no use coming over here, putting a boring old applique koala on something and expecting some department-store buyer to jump up and down with glee. I mean, she's not really interested.'

Nor are her customers back in Australia. In an interesting twist, the David Jones store in Sydney improved sales of her garments by moving them away from other local products and putting them on display with imported fashions. She approves: 'It's nice to be treated as if you're an international company, rather than just a local designer.'

When he started out in business, Sir Peter Abeles would have been happy with a million-dollar business like Anne Lewin's. 'My original plan when I started in 1950 with two trucks . . . was to have a hundred trucks,' he said in mid-1989. By then, his trucks were counted in the thousands and his turnover was well over $3 billion. TNT, the freight and transport company of which he is chief executive, delivers its services in 85 countries and has 700 offices throughout the world and about 60 000 employees. It is effectively establishing a truly global transport network which cuts across east-west boundaries in a way unmatched by any other aviation or freight organisation.

The story of the rise of Peter Abeles to one of the most prominent positions in Australian business has been covered in other publications: born in Vienna and brought up in Budapest; escape from a German labour camp during World War II; flight from Hungary and impending communist rule after the war; migration to Australia in 1949; takeover by Thomas Nationwide Transport in 1967 but with Abeles becoming chief executive of the new company; establishment of TNT operations in Europe, North and South America, and Asia; takeover of Ansett Transport Industries, which operates Australia's major commercial airline, with Rupert Murdoch.

His career has had its controversial aspects, ranging from his close relationship with Labor Prime Minister Bob Hawke to environmental complaints over the building of a monorail in Sydney. Through it all, he has pressed on with developing diverse but synergised transport interests involving ships, aircraft, trucks and trains.

It is too big a story to describe in detail in these pages, but two recent developments highlight TNT's success in moving into overseas markets. The first is its rapid domination of European air express services. The second is that it has now taken those services into Eastern Europe.

TNT has been active in Europe for more than a decade. It began operations in the UK in 1978 when it bought a local company, Inter County Express. Don Dick, now TNT Europe's Chief Executive, remembers what 'express' services were like in the UK at that time. 'I just found that there were absolutely no marketing ideas, no sales people, no aggression whatsoever, no innovation,' he says. 'The product was a three-day delivery product in England. No one ever dreamt it could be done any other way.'

The new product which TNT introduced into the UK in 1980 was overnight service. 'Express' suddenly meant next-day delivery. Dick remembers the attitudes of TNT's competitors in the UK: 'It took three or four years for them to really believe that what we were talking about and what we were marketing was, in fact, working . . . They were very sceptical but they soon got on the bandwagon after that. But we had such a huge lead on them [that], as soon as they looked like catching up, we were away developing new products.'

TNT now has 35 divisional companies operating in the UK where it employs more than 7000 people. The service they offer range from same-day to three-day freight delivery, parcel delivery and courier services to newspaper distribution for Rupert Murdoch, TNT Mailfast, which aims to outspeed international postal deliveries, and so on. By 1989, the company was earning nearly $A13 million a week in the UK. To improve its competitive edge, it opened in the same year a 19 acre (7.7 hectare) 'sortation complex' at Atherstone near Birmingham; among other things, it can handle up to 12 000 parcels an hour.

Through a combination of the development of its own operations and the takeover of existing facilities, TNT spread beyond the UK into the rest of Western Europe. Its trucks now operate from its own freight centres scattered strategically across the continent. The long-term goal has been to provide next-day deliveries to every town and city in Western Europe.

Both the pursuit of that goal and the satisfaction of TNT's initial Eastern European ambitions have as a common denominator a new type of aircraft acquired in a spectacular buying coup. The aircraft is the freight version of an established British Aerospace four-engined fan-jet airliner. It is called the 146 Quiet Trader—in aviation shorthand, the BAe 146-QT. It is regarded as the world's quietest jet, has excellent short take-off and landing capabilities, has established its reliability and delivers an ideal payload of about 12 tonnes of freight and in containerised form for quick turnaround.

The biggest of its various attractions was that it could operate comfortably within the night-time noise limitations of European airports. Until it came along, no manufacturer anywhere was producing a jet freighter that could do this. 'When we established our European express operations . . . we knew that noise curfews at airports, together with the environmental lobby of organisations such as the Green Party, would be a major factor in anything we decided to do,' Neil Hansford, the Managing Director of TNT International Aviation Services, has told a British aerospace journal. 'It was immediately apparent that the crunch would be to find a good neighbourly aircraft with which we could operate an unrestricted night service.'

There were only two such aircraft—the Boeing 737-300 and the BAe 146, which, in its passenger configuration, was known as the Whispering Jet. But Boeing told TNT that it wasn't interested in making a freight version of the 737-300. British Aerospace, however, was very interested. Indeed, it was prepared to work with TNT personnel to come up with a freight version of the 146 which would meet the transportation company's detailed needs.

TNT had found what it wanted. In 1986 it placed orders and options for 72 of the 146-QTs—British Aerospace's entire production of the aircraft until 1992. The total cost of the deal was $2.1 billion. Thirty of the jets are being phased into its European express freight network. The rest will be marketed through Ansett Worldwide Aviation Services, a subsidiary of Ansett Transport Industries.

Until the filling of those orders or until another manufacturer comes along with an equivalent to the BAe 146-QT, TNT has effectively cornered the market in this type of aircraft. *British Aerospace Business Review* announced in 1989: 'TNT, already the world's largest transportation organisation, finds itself No. 1 in European express airfreight league as well.' Don Dick says European-based and owned carriers 'are more than a little upset' and 'are light years behind the system that we now have in place'.

The filling of TNT's current orders for the 146-QT will coincide with the unification of the Western European market in 1992. It is a significant coincidence. 'TNT already had a sophisticated express road delivery system in Europe,' Neil Hansford says. 'But we knew that in the run up to 1992, Europe would begin to expect the same service levels that have long been available in the USA and South Pacific . . . A mature European single market will require up to 30 aircraft to enable us consistently to pick up from our customers by six in the evening and deliver, customs cleared, by nine the next morning anywhere in Europe— and that includes the non-EEC countries. Twelve months ago the overnight express industry in Europe was a decade behind North America and Australia but the tremendous rate of acceleration since then is likely to see it catch up by 1990.'

By mid-1989, TNT had 14 BAe 146-QTs operating in Europe. The hub of their operations is Cologne, West Germany. Each night, the aircraft fly there from the UK Ireland, France, Spain, Austria, Italy, Finland, Sweden Norway, Denmark, Switzerland, elsewhere in West Germany and from Budapest, the capital of Hungary. Containers are transferred between the planes which then fly on to their desinations.

That single plane from Budapest was TNT's first toehold in the East European bloc. It is operated by TNT-Malev Express Cargo Ltd, a joint venture set up by TNT, Hungary' national airline, Malev, and Hungarian trading and bank interests; TNT's share of the venture is 40 per cent. This deal represents two important breakthroughs: the 146-QT is the first Western transport aircraft to be delivered to Hungary since the end of World War II; and it is Malev's first joint venture with the West.

Given Sir Peter Abeles' origins, it is perhaps not surprising that his company's first eastward move in Europe should be to Hungary. His homeland has been in the forefront of the political, social and economic changes which have characterised the Gorbachev era in much of Eastern Europe. Part of the process has been an attempt to put aside the repressive prejudices of earlier periods of communist rule. One example has been the recasting of the image of disgraced former Premier, Imre Nagy, the most public victim of the Soviet Union's crushing of the 1956 Hungarian uprising against Russian domination. Another has been a new toleration of Hungarians who fled to the West to escape communism. The current official tendency is not to see them as some kind of traitor but as people who were seeking financial opportunities not available in Hungary at the time.

When Sir Peter went back to Hungary in the lead-up to the signing of the TNT-Malev deal in October 1988, he was greeted with more than toleration. He was welcomed home like a long-lost son. As one TNT staffer points out, for a country with few post-war success stories to tell, 'he may well have become the richest Hungarian in the world'.

Not that he describes himself as being especially Hungarian any longer. Australia is his home and the world is place of business. Besides, as he spent his very first years in Vienna, he has lived only 12 years of his entire life in Hungary. Despite that, his first trip back to Budapest was 'naturally an emotional experience' he says. 'I went to my old high school; I went to the place where my parents lived, and a few other places which brought back memories.' But some of the nostalgia has passed and he now regards trips to Budapest as 'more a business situation than emotional'.

As for his hosts, he believes that his continued fluency in Hungarian—a language which bears no similarity to any other, apart from Finnish—helps. 'They regard me as an

Australian who knows the country and therefore they feel comfortable because they don't have to explain to me and they can communicate with me without interpreters.'

Each night, the TNT-Malev 146-QT takes off from Budapest Airport about 8 pm, flies to Linz in Austria and then on to Cologne. It often goes on to Luton in England to help lift UK airfreight across the Channel. By dawn, it is back in Budapest with parcels ready for delivery that morning. Parked on the tarmac at Budapest Airport, it stands out—partly because of the distinctive yellow and black colours which it has carried on from TNT and partly because most of the Malev fleet consists of Russian aircraft (although the airline is now also leasing three Boeing 737s for passenger flights).

The person charged with introducing the express delivery system to Hungary is TNT executive Chris Greensides. He moved to Budapest from China, where he had played a similar troubleshooting role in getting TNT services off the ground. He found that Hungary had published schedules in which deliveries took up to 12 days. The concept of overnight delivery was quite novel. Through 1989, he worked at overcoming that novelty.

On his side was a growing awareness among Hungarians that they need to sell more of their goods in the West— a reversal of the existing direction of trade. 'A lot of their products are going towards Russia,' he says. 'They're paid in roubles. It's useless as far as [hard] foreign currency is concerned, so they've got to look to the West to seek their contracts to earn a big dollar.' His job is to persuade them that express airfreight can be a cost-effective way of helping to earn that dollar.

It was a slow start in Hungary but worth some patience. It helped put TNT in a better position than any of its competitors to exploit new freight opportunities in the Eastern bloc. While getting TNT-Malev underway, its executives were already holding discussions with Soviet officials. Organisationally, they had the example of TNT-Malev to show how TNT can make joint East-West venture work.

Sir Peter Abeles says TNT is not going into Eastern Europe

'for the sake of growing'. An enormous market is opening up and the best way to service its customers is for TNT to go in first, he believes. In his 40 years in transport, one thing has always been true: 'If you offer your service, then, all of a sudden, trade follows that service, and trade—unexpected even if it may be in an area—starts to develop. So you can't be second. You can't first watch the trade and then develop the service. If you do that, then you are a follower and TNT, I think, always tries to be a leader and that's why we are in the eastern market.'

In August 1989, only two months after Sir Peter recorded those comments, TNT took its most important leap into the Eastern bloc. It signed an agreement with Aeroflot—the world's biggest airline, the Russian flag carrier and the umbrella organisation for every civilian flight in the USSR—to introduce a door-to-door express courier service in the Soviet Union. Thus, a carrier of Australian origin has become the first Western freight operator to be allowed to operate in the USSR.

From September 1989, TNT Aeroflot Express Services began operating from Moscow Airport as a critical new leg in the worldwide network of TNT Skypak, the organisation's international courier service. Collection points were established in Moscow, Leningrad and Kiev to enable companies and organisations operating in the Soviet Union to dispatch urgent material to the outside world.

The Eastern and Western European developments took place against a more-or-less simultaneous background of expansionist activity by TNT and its related company, Ansett Transport Industries, in other parts of the world, particularly South America. In August 1989, Sir Peter told the *Australian Financial Review* that it was 'an absolute goal' eventually to link all of his international freight operations, either with TNT or Ansett aircraft, or through other carriers. The multiplicity of his recent deals led Eric Ellis, of the *Sydney Morning Herald,* to comment a few days later: 'Australia already has a second international airline to rival Qantas in form, if not function. Significantly, Air Abeles is everywhere the Australian flag carrier is not.'

The Australian products described in this chapter share certain features. Either they or early forms of them were developed and proven in Australia before they were taken overseas. This is true even of EOS which, superficially, has the characteristics of an overnight success: the key personnel had worked together in the same technological area for the Australian Government for years before they decided to apply their skills commercially in the global marketplace. Anne Lewin had perfected her lingerie in the local market; TNT had honed its express freight concepts and practices here; and the McKay group, above all, had chipped away at the conservatism of railway engineers before achieving their first contractual acceptance by the Australian National Railways.

Despite that domestic start, all of the merchandise products—those of EOS, McKay and Anne Lewin—had to be taken overseas if they were to find significant sales. Indeed, EOS laser ranging systems and McKay's Safelok clip would not have been worth developing commercially without their overseas sales and Anne Lewin's lingerie would have had to struggle along in a very small market. In the services sector, TNT might have been a good profitable business without overseas expansion but it would have been a fraction of its current size and quite possibly a takeover target for the very kind of international operator which it has become

It is also evident that all the product lines have resulted from their producers' commitment to innovation, or, in the case of Anne Lewin, to revitalisation of an old indulgence This gave TNT and McKay the edge they needed when they took on huge overseas markets against formidable challengers. It provided Anne Lewin's niche. And it has been Ben Greene's 'ace in the hole'.

Laurie Carmichael, of the ACTU, identifies quality and uniqueness as key factors which Australian products must have to make it in the modern world market. TNT might be, in Sir Peter Abeles' words, 'just a carrier' but it organisation and methods have set it apart from it competitors; and EOS, McKay and Anne Lewin have al emphasised the quality and distinctiveness of their products

Carmichael explains the importance of these factors: 'Th market today has changed in quite a dramatic fashion . .

Quality and uniqueness, warranty, durability—these are factors that are predominant in the world market. Twenty years ago, everybody was still looking for the lowest priced, lowest cost product . . . Without uniqueness of product, there is no niche for any nation. Every nation has the right to a slice of the world action but there is no corporate body out there in the world that will allocate your slice. You have to get it yourself and the only way you can get it is to ensure that you have uniqueness that attracts a proportion of that world market.'

Sir Peter Abeles emphasises quality, too: 'Whatever we do—whether we're in the manufacturing industry or the mining industry or in the service industry—we have to think, first, quality, because to compete in the world we have to have quality. Then, when we have it, we have to get out and not sit at home and look for others to sell our products. We have to get out and sell it ourselves and this applies, in my opinion, not only to large operations like ours but it applies to small and medium sized operations. You only have to look at countries like Italy, Switzerland, Holland, and I could go on. There are a number of small countries who for generations have found their place in the big world, well before the Common Market was ever discovered . . . That's what we have to do now: become part of the world and have something to sell which is acceptable by the world and then ram it down every customer's throat.'

Tokyo-based Senior Trade Commissioner Greg Dodds draws an important distinction between the price and the value of a product. He says countries like the United States and Australia have put a lot of emphasis in the last decade or so into containing or reducing the cost of products to the consumer. 'That's fine as far as it goes, of course, but in some cases I think the value has suffered as a result,' he says. 'What people have to look at when they come to Japan is getting on the Japanese wavelength which is to develop the value—to up the value and, if the value goes up, so can the price.' He tells of Australian manufacturers who, when consulting AUSTRADE's Tokyo office, have stressed that they have kept a product cheap by applying a 'no-frills' approach to it. 'The first thing that comes to my mind is: why no frills? You should be perhaps thinking about more frills. Frills are what give the extra price, the market advantage.'

To Dodds, packaging is the biggest frill of the lot. 'Quality packaging or the lack of it can mean the difference between a product exciting the interest of not only the consumer but, before the consumer, the wholesaler, the retailer . . . and the product being put aside. So packaging is the vehicle that will carry it to the right point in the market system.'

Professor Jim Montague, Professor of Industrial Design at Sydney's University of Technology, also points to Japanese criticism of the packaging of Australian products: 'I think a difference between the two cultures is that the package and opening the package is a much more ceremonial and important activity to the Japanese than it is to us. We sort of rip the package off, throw it aside and get at the product. For the Japanese, the entire process is part of the product itself. If we're not sensitive to that, we can produce some very good quality products which will sit on the shelf.'

For Montague, this is part of the much wider issue of the attitude of Australians to design. It has been estimated that only one in ten Australian manufacturers use professional designers to design their products. This function is most often left to such people as the chief engineer or the managing director's wife. Yet it is vital: the designer's maxim is that, given equal performance and equal price, people will always buy the better-looking product.

3 Marketing

Heard the one about the Tasmanian calendar salesman who had been turned down by a dozen potential Japanese customers? 'I don't understand these Japanese,' he said. 'What more could they want? These calendars have got everything: Moomba Day, Queen's Birthday, Anzac Day, the lot.' Sydney Morning Herald, 26 August 1989

THE story has to be apocryphal. But it serves to highlight the ignorance of some Australian business people about the Japanese market. It also indicates blindness to the broader point: a product which is perfect for the domestic market can be a complete failure overseas.

Those Australians are not alone in their blindness. Dr Jane C. Munro, a senior lecturer in the School of Commerce at the University of New South Wales, relates a less obviously crass American mistake: 'When they tried to market instant cake mixes into the Japanese market, they hit on the idea that every Japanese house had an automatic rice cooker and that automatic rice cooker could be used to make an instant cake. They found the Japanese housewives wouldn't buy it. What they [the Americans] didn't know was that the rice cooker in Japan is almost like a ritually pure object and the Japanese housewife would never put anything but rice in her rice cooker.'

Further examples from Dr Munro: 'The Americans couldn't market big cars into Japan and they didn't know why. The fact is that Japanese streets are too narrow for big cars. You just can't sell them. You can't market big fridges into Japan because they don't have big spaces in their houses for those fridges, and Japanese housewives want to shop every day, not once or twice a week.'

However good a product, there can be a gap between it and its potential consumers. What can bridge that gap— or save time and money by showing that it is unbridgeable— is marketing. Lindsay MacAlister, Managing Director of AUSTRADE, defines its importance for Australian manufacturers: 'The classic challenge that we face is that of marketing—that is, anticipating, identifying and satisfying needs in foreign markets profitably in the face of acutely intensifying competition.'

Some Australian manufacturers think marketing is a cheap and simple exercise, as Greg Dodds, Senior Australian Trade Commissioner in Tokyo, shows: 'We often get these letters from Australia just asking us to send them a list of people who might import [particular products]—the notion being that you send us these names and addresses and we'll write off to them and that should do the trick. What's been invested in that process is not much more than a postage stamp. The chances of a successful purchase resulting from that in Japan . . . are practically nil.'

Others confuse marketing with selling. Dr Munro explains why the terms are not interchangeable: 'Selling is just a process which is part of an over-arching activity called marketing. Marketing means thinking first and foremost about the market that you want to enter, the people who want to buy something that you might want to make. If you have a product that will suit that market, then you're going to be able to sell it. The selling of the product itself is really just the mechanism to get the product into the market.'

Marketing has a number of aspects. Dr Munro stresses the need for exporters 'to understand the real nature of their market' and adds: 'This is why market research is very important; why studying the environment of the market is important; why studying the profiles of the people concerned in the market is very important—the preferences of the consumers . . . [and] the kinds of images those consumers will respond to . . .'

Many things can flow from this beginning. Marketing

can identify a niche into which a product will fit. It might mean modifying a product to suit consumer preferences or at least stressing some of its characteristics over others. It will encompass the positioning of a product in a market; projecting a positive image of the product; and so on. In short, marketing is the means of matching products with their consumers.

This chapter looks at four Australian products and the way in which the people behind them have understood the importance of marketing.

The first shows how marketing techniques are turning a proverbial sow's ear into a silk purse. This might seem an odd application of the old metaphor since the product, diamonds, normally conjures up images of great wealth. But not all diamonds are equally valuable. The Argyle diamond mine in the Kimberley region of Western Australia demonstrated this point well: it had many millions of carats of diamonds but only about 5 per cent were of gem quality; the rest were destined for industrial use or were what the trade calls 'cheap gems'. Argyle is dealing with its peculiar challenges by pursuing a multi-level marketing policy with very interesting results.

David Livingstone is a Sydney accountant who, bored with his profession, invented a new machine to look after the turf on golf courses, grass tennis courts, even football fields. He knew he had a superior product but he faced the problem of convincing greenkeepers around the world. He decided that the best way to do this was first to gain acceptance in some of the premier locations in the world. Now, his machine is being snapped up in some unlikely places.

Melbourne company Beecham Beverages has achieved overseas success with what many would consider a very ordinary product—mineral water flavoured with natural fruit juices. But behind that success have been painstakingly careful market research and promotional activities. A marketing man's marketing man, managing director John Chatham has used all of these tools not only to launch his product overseas but to keep it in a leading market position.

Finally, Colin Dangaard, a former journalist from Sydney, has achieved a 'coals-to-Newcastle' success by selling

Australian saddles into the American West. He has had the advantage of some high-profile customers and he has cleverly adapted his product to suit his new market.

What unites John Chatham and Colin Dangaard is the way in which they have both cashed in on American curiosity about Australia after the success of such movies as *The Man from Snowy River* and *Crocodile Dundee*.

It is no coincidence that two of the exporters profiled in this chapter are not professional marketers. AUSTRADE's Lindsay MacAlister points out that 'we are relatively new to the business of marketing consumer-type products'. We trained engineers, scientists and accountants but 'didn't have a compelling need to train marketing people'. Now, when we need them most, they are not always there and we have to rely on the improvisation of inspired individuals.

Diamonds were found in Australia as long ago as 1851, but they remained oddities in this otherwise mineral-rich country. By the 1920s, a few minor fields had yielded only about 200 000 carats. That is about 40 kilograms—less than the weight of an apprentice jockey. While sporadic prospecting continued, the outlook was gloomy. 'No one ever thought diamonds were a likely possibility in this part of the world, except for those of us who were searching inside Australia,' says David Karpin, Managing Director of Argyle Diamonds.

Even for the optimists, it was hard going. A joint venture, the forerunner of Karpin's company, was formed in 1972 to explore the potential of the Kimberley region of north-west Australia. It is a remote, sparsely populated area where temperatures can climb to 50°C. In these conditions, prospecting was very expensive and, by 1976, the joint venturers had to take on a wealthy partner, Conzinc Rio Tinto Australia (CRA). CRA now effectively controls 60 per cent of the company, with the rest in the hands of Ashton Mining Limited, a publicly listed corporation in which Malaysia Mining Corporation Berhad has a 46 per cent stake.

It is a remarkable coincidence that the region in which they searched has the same name as the great Kimberley diamond mine in South Africa. For, in 1979, the joint venturers found what they were looking for: a 'pipe', a deposit of volcanic rock, in which commercial quantities of diamonds were imbedded, plus alluvial deposits of the precious gems. The joint venturers began mining the alluvials in 1983 and the pipe in December 1985.

They call it the Argyle pipe and it is bigger than any mine in South Africa. Or anywhere. It takes 100 tonnes of rock at Argyle to produce just seven carats of diamonds, less than a gram and a half. But it is producing more than 30 million carats a year. That is one third of the world's diamonds. And its proven reserves will sustain mining for at least 20 years.

Outsiders would expect the immense deposits to keep smiles on the corporate faces of the joint venturers for just as long. And it would be wrong to say the prospectors were unhappy with their discovery. But the Argyle discovery posed a number of problems which had to be overcome before it could return anything like the profits for which they were hoping.

All the problems had marketing implications. They required just the sort of multi-level, innovative thinking for which the joint venturers formed their own marketing company, Argyle Diamond Sales (ADS).

ADS organises the sale of most Argyle diamonds through an offshoot of the legendary De Beers Organisation. De Beers Consolidated Mines, a multinational financial, industrial, engineering and mining conglomerate, has diamond mining interests in South Africa (which now contributes only about 10 per cent of the world's stones), Botswana and Namibia. More importantly, it dominates the world diamond trade, especially through its London-based distribution, marketing and research arm, the Central Selling Organisation (CSO).

But ADS does not sell all its diamonds through CSO. Instead, it markets directly those stones that need special handling. Sometimes, these are very rare and very, very valuable. Sometimes, ADS must seek to maximise the market potential of diamonds which might otherwise be dismissed as being of relatively little value—and Argyle has a lot of diamonds which need this treatment.

Behind this need is Argyle's first problem: not many of

its diamonds are white. And, according to David Karpin, when Argyle stones came on to the market, 'white diamonds were the be-all and end-all of diamonds'. Whites are overwhelmingly the stones which are traditionally described as gems. On average, about 17 per cent of the output of the world's mines are classed as gems. That is where the big money is. Of the rest, about 40 per cent of diamonds are graded as 'cheap gems' and 43 per cent as 'industrials' —to be used as the cutting edge on machine tools.

Argyle is out of kilter with these percentages. Only 5 per cent of its diamonds are gems, 45 per cent are cheap gems and 50 per cent are industrials. And the great majority of its diamonds are brown and small. If Argyle had committed itself simply to selling all of its stones through the CSO, its returns would have been permanently inhibited by their unfashionable colour and size. So ADS decided to set out to change a centuries-old fashion to enable it to get its plain old browns into the world's best jewellery shops. For that, it needed a totally new marketing concept.

'Colour and international became the catch cries at Argyle,' Karpin says, 'so that we looked for an international figure to work with us to get this concept across, and we selected Stuart Devlin, who's the Queen's Goldsmith. He had a number of factors going for him. He was Australian, he was worldwide in reputation and he had a sympathy for the task we'd set ourselves.'

Stuart Devlin—the person who designed Australia's first decimal coins—moved to England in 1965. In 1980, he was granted 'the Royal Warrant of Appointment as Goldsmith and Jeweller to Her Majesty the Queen'. He now lives and works in a classic English country-garden setting in Surrey. His commission from Argyle cast him in a multiple role— marketer, ideas man and designer.

He sums up the task he faced: 'There is no [gem] market for brown diamonds, whereas, with De Beers, they started from a market which was already established for white diamonds. People were very fascinated by these sparkling white stones . . . De Beers have done a fabulous job in developing that interest and that romance. What we had to do was start from scratch and develop an interest in something that people weren't interested in.'

Devlin was interested in them. 'They're incredibly beautiful,' he says, 'so I thought there must be something one can do with them.' But it was not easy. The stones fell into two groups: dark brown and light brown. At first, he found it hard, when he set them, to show them off to advantage. 'It was a real disaster,' he recalls, 'and that was my first job as a consultant for Argyle and they weren't terribly happy with me having to abort a program that they had spent a lot of money on.'

Then, he tried yellow-gold settings for the diamonds. He was delighted with the result. The darker browns produced an intense contrast with the gold while the lighter browns merged with its yellowness. So he set about designing an exhibition of jewellery ranging from rings to intricate mechanised 'eggs', descendants of the work of the great Russian jeweller, Faberge. The exhibition, in Britain and Australia in 1987–88, was an immense success and attracted considerable attention in the media and, importantly, in the trade.

Devlin had done more than put the diamonds in the right settings: he also renamed them. 'Within the trade, brown is a dirty word and it wasn't a very romantic word,' he says. Instead, he called them 'champagne' and 'cognac' diamonds—champagne for the lighter browns and cognac for the darker ones. David Karpin sees it as a breakthrough: 'We've got the trade thinking in new terms. Champagne and cognac is a much more acceptable and saleable concept than dim, dark, dank brown.'

Devlin also created new styles of jewellery. He particularly points to the champagne diamond settings as being suited to more informal wear than white diamonds. 'These diamonds could well be worn, for instance, by what we might call the career or business woman who is becoming a very, very powerful influence in the marketplace. And you can't really envisage those sorts of sophisticated people wearing white diamonds during the daytime. They tend to wear plain yellow gold or pearls or something like that. But now . . . they can wear champagne diamond jewellery.' In addition, he thinks they appeal to younger people, who traditionally have only bought white diamonds in engagement rings.

Argyle has yet to launch the champagne and cognac diamonds into the two biggest markets—the United States and Japan. 'With a move like that, you get only one chance, so we want to get it right,' an Argyle executive says. The stakes are high. If the project succeeds, it will transform the price of the better-quality and bigger browns and make the joint venturers very much wealthier.

Stuart Devlin's ideas affect the finest of the champagne and cognac stones. But, for many other Argyle browns, the best prospects are in the booming diamond market of India. India, where diamonds were first discovered more than two centuries before Christ, has come back into its own in recent years as a diamond-cutting centre. More than one million people are employed in the industry there and they handle six out of ten of the world's diamonds.

Behind India's resurgence has been a spectacular growth in demand for inexpensive, mass-produced jewellery using diamonds of 'cheap gem' quality. It can only be made by labour that is both skilled and cheap. India can provide it. But here Argyle encountered yet another problem: many Indian craftsmen found it hard to cut Argyle browns as easily as stones from other sources. On realising this, Argyle virtually took its marketing to the factory floor: it decided to put considerable effort into easing the craftsmen's task.

The major difficulty was with equipment. The right sort of equipment had been priced beyond reach by high Indian customs tariffs. So Argyle decided to provide technical and financial assistance for the equipment to be manufactured in India and for existing equipment to be adapted. A key to the new or modified equipment is the use of brown-diamond grit from Argyle in cutting and polishing. It is busily promoting the technology wherever possible. At one trade show at Surat, north of Bombay, it flew in a Belgian hard-stone specialist from its Perth factory to show how to handle stones previously considered unpolishable. Argyle won the show's main prize for technology.

Effecting the change is a slow process but it is worth the effort because of India's importance in a growing sector of world demand for diamonds. It is another example of how Argyle has taken a multi-level approach to marketing. So far, with export revenue running above $300 million, it is paying off.

Making a contribution to that figure out all proportion to their size or numbers are Argyle pink diamonds. They are exceedingly scarce: only 60 to 90 carats are extracted every year. That's just two to three carats in every million. The best of the pinks are sold directly by ADS. Not only has this helped achieve very high prices but it has created a kind of brand awareness of Argyle.

Previously, pink diamonds had been found in only a few of the world's mines and never in quantities exceeding a few carats a year. They have also generally been very light in colour and have looked even paler when set in jewellery. The world has never had a reliable source for the kind of pink diamonds that come from Argyle. They have a unique intensity of colour, with some so deep that they verge on red.

Argyle sold its first pinks by tender in 1986, 1987 and 1988. Then, in 1989, ADS took a very bold step. It decided to sell a collection of prize pinks by public auction at Christie's New York. The 16 pinks weighed a total 19.51 carats—less than four grams—and the biggest was 3.14 carats. The auction was a huge success with the bids reaching as high as $1 million a carat.

But it was not the prices alone that made the auction so unusual. It was also the fact that it was held at all. For this was the first time a diamond producer had taken its stones directly to the public auction rooms. It put Argyle on the map. 'We've done things in the international marketplace that have brought attention to us and that attention has been very positive and something that has led us to be recognised as an integral part of the diamond world,' David Karpin says.

The optimism inspired by the success of the pinks and by the hopes for the champagne and cognac stones contrast with the circumstances attending the advent of Argyle diamonds. The 1970s had seen a speculative boom in diamonds as a result of a government-inspired demand 'bubble' in Israel. But, just as the extraordinary size of the Argyle pipe was being established in 1980, the bubble burst.

The price was still healthy when judged from a ten-year perspective and the boom-and-bust phenomenon had largely occurred at the very top end of the range. The market overall proved remarkably resilient. This was in no small part due to the efforts of De Beers and CSO, its marketing arm. CSO stabilised the market, first by temporarily reducing sale stocks and then by continuing to open up a vast new source of well-heeled consumers—Japan.

Its Japanese success is one of the marketing triumphs of modern times. The Japanese have no tradition of precious stones. Now, person for person, they buy more polished diamonds than any other people on earth. CSO played a large part in inducing this change through a sustained advertising and promotional campaign.

But dealers and investors were feeling shaky as the Argyle mine came on stream. And, among pessimistic observers, the new arrival was like a monster which would devour the whole industry and itself. One commentator argued that 'this plethora of diamonds . . . will probably signal the final collapse of world diamond prices', in which event 'the diamond invention will disintegrate and be remembered only as a historical curiosity'.

He was wrong. One of the reasons was that Argyle opted for the advantages of an orderly market by submitting most of its diamonds for sale through the CSO. Whatever the temptation to try to go it alone, Argyle saw greater benefits in largely fitting in with the existing system. 'De Beers are a very positive force in the world diamond industry and working with them has brought an association that brings us attention and acceptance,' David Karpin says. So linking up with De Beers' CSO became 'the first move' in Argyle's marketing strategy.

But, as we have seen, Argyle did not entirely submit to the old system. Instead, it has used it as a base from which it has moved to create its own independent market opportunities. With its own cutting and polishing operation, for which it has imported expert technicians, in Perth, and a sales office, from which it markets about one-quarter of

Argyle's output, in Antwerp, Belgium, ADS is making some unusual moves in what has been a very tightly-controlled industry.

At 32, David Livingstone, a Sydney accountant, was running a finance company. But he felt he had nowhere else to go and was getting bored. Then, on a Sunday afternoon, he went to a neighbourhood barbecue which led to a complete change in his life.

His host 'had a couple of weird contraptions in his garage that I knew nothing about,' he recalls. 'He said they were turf aerators and, after a little bit more prodding and a few more beers, I found out they actually punched holes in the ground and that was an essential operation for greenkeeping.' By punching holes in turf, aerators help water and other nutrients to get down to the roots of the grass on golfing greens, lawn tennis courts and other sporting grounds. Livingstone's neighbour had a business in which he used his machines to service sporting turf surfaces around Sydney.

A few months later, Livingstone decided to leave his comfortable job and go out on his own. Simultaneously, he discovered that his neighbour wanted to sell his business. 'So I acquired his turf aeration business and he gave me his tax work,' he says. 'The whole idea then was that my tax work would be starting off from scratch and it would be supplemented by the turf aeration business. But eventually the turf aeration business just took over everything.'

From 1980 to 1984, Livingstone ran his business, Greencare, hiring out the machinery and his own operators. He came to realise why greenkeepers always hired—never bought—aerators: 'Nobody wanted the maintenance problems . . . I could not believe that an industry which is so critical, such as sports turf, had to put up with this sort of machinery . . . it was so bad.'

Livingstone decided to invent a better machine. And he did: 'It became a classic [case of] necessity being the mother of invention. I was after a machine which would do the job four times faster with no maintenance problems and it required not only a new design but an entirely new approach to the problem. All turf aerators of the day were stand-alone units, so they had their own gasoline engine and their own hydraulic system . . . So we hit upon the idea of putting a turf aerator behind a tractor . . . The tractor itself would power the unit and the tractor's hydraulic system would lift and lower the unit. So we eliminated two-thirds of the mechanical problems and we increased the maintenance reliability approximately 200 per cent.'

He called his new aerating unit the Coremaster 12. It was clearly a good machine and, when he launched it on the Australian market in 1985, it took off. In a greenkeeping community the size of Australia's, word-of-mouth quickly spread its reputation around the country. But that very matter of size—or the lack of it—meant he would soon face the problem of market saturation. To get the full commercial benefit of his invention, he would have to export it overseas.

But how would he market it? It is, after all, not a very flash product. How could he grab the attention of overseas greenkeepers and convince them of its superiority? The answer lay in a clever marketing strategy: if he could sell Coremaster to the most prestigious sporting locations, the groundsmen of the world would follow.

First, he tested the water by taking Coremaster to the United States for the Golf Course Superintendent's Show. It stole the show: interest was so intense that security guards insisted he close his booth several times to enable the crowd to disperse.

Trade shows, then and now, are an integral part of Livingstone's marketing tactics. He attends three a year. 'Trade shows are very important because you don't necessarily sell a machine at a trade show—you actually wave the flag and establish your credibility,' he says. 'If you have a large stand with lots of activity and lots of videos, people feel comfortable with your product, particularly when it's a new one, and particularly when it's made as far away as in Australia. You get a lot of contacts; you've got to have back-up with brochures and export price lists; you've got to do your homework well. And the leads you get out of them and the leads you get from the leads are excellent. We also use AUSTRADE extensively for back-up research

Livingstone concentrated his early efforts on the United States. The statistics explain that decision: there are 20 000 golf courses in the US, compared to 2000 in Australia. But it was a bold move into the heartland of the enemy. For the US is the source of the great majority of the greenkeeping equipment.

Livingstone established Greencare International in Los Angeles as an independent company to cater to the US, Canadian and Caribbean markets and eventually to arrange dealerships. And Greencare set about getting Coremaster accepted in the best places. It was slow at first: in 1985–86, fewer than 20 Coremasters were sold in the US. But those first sales seeded the market. The following year, 140 American sales were made and, in the year after that, about 220. At around $18 000 for each unit (including the small tractor), the sales—for a relatively new, suburban Sydney company—were looking good.

More importantly, most of the top 100 golf courses in the United States bought the machine. And Coremaster's uses went beyond golfing greens: it groomed the ground surface at two American Superbowl football finals. Those were the credentials Livingstone wanted so he could move into other markets.

When he went to the UK, he continued his strategy of starting at the top. Not surprisingly, he targeted Wimbledon, still the most prestigious tennis venue in the world. Head groundsman Jim Thorn explains what that means: 'The people in this country expect by right that this should be supreme, should look supreme, and we've got to do this. So any available equipment that's going that can help us we'll get and we'll use it. We've got probably a reputation second to none; we're proud of our reputation . . .

'Price mustn't enter into it. If the machine is right, no matter what it costs, we will buy it. Not everybody can do this . . . All the other groundsmen are looking to us to try new equipment out. We can afford it; they can't afford to try it and make a mistake. They will listen to us because we are accepted people . . . They'll ring me up. This goes on all the time and it doesn't just come from this country strangely enough. It comes from all over the world . . . You produce a good machine, we'll use it and we'll say it's good. If it's bad, we'll say it's bad.'

Fortunately for David Livingstone, Jim Thorn tells everyone that Coremaster is a good machine. He lists a number of technical advantages and stresses its reliability. Wimbledon had previously used American equipment but, says Thorn, it was too complicated and sophisticated: 'If it went wrong, we knew darn well we had a three-month breakdown period. We had to wait three months for spares to get it going again. Big problems. When Coremaster came along, it's robust. I mean that's putting it mildly. It's more than robust. If it broke down, you give it a damn great hit with a sledgehammer and it will go again. There is no problem.'

All the work Livingstone had put in at the developmental stage to reduce the number of working parts in his aerator from 400 to 12 essential pieces was paying off. He got the same positive reaction at Sunningdale, one of Britain's top golf courses. And so Coremaster was sold to other prestigious locations, such as St Andrew's and Gleneagles.

Apart from a few sales to France through an English distributor, Livingstone had not tried to penetrate the European market before 1989. And then, in choosing the first country in which to make a concerted effort, he made what might seem like a strange choice: Sweden.

Like many people, Livingstone thought of Sweden mainly as a land of ice and snow, with a summer too short for the encouragement of such outdoor sports as golf. But, at a trade show, he was approached by a Swedish company which thought their home country would provide a worthwhile market for Coremaster. 'We thought Sweden was a very small country and we'd never put it on the map,' Livingstone says. 'We did our market research and found that there are 200 golf courses now, with another 150 planned . . . What's amazing is that the golf-course industry in Sweden has trebled in the last 20 years and it looks like that sort of expansion will continue . . .

'The history of golf in Sweden is a little bit different to Europe and America because, until very recently, golf in Sweden was a very exclusive sport. But now everybody' getting involved in it, [including] whole families. You haven't got the structures like in England and America where it's very regimented. In Sweden, everybody's here to enjoy themselves and it's really good to see that with a family-orientated sport.'

In May 1989, Livingstone flew to Malmo in southern Sweden, where, with the country's mildest climate, most golf is played. There, he concluded a distribution deal with Am-Cani, the company whose representatives had spotted Coremaster at the trade show. (They admit now that they had initially thought the machine was American.) Am-Cani is an ideal distributor: it has been marketing agricultural machinery throughout southern Sweden for more than a century; as it has diversified into the booming golf industry, it has had the advantage of a long-established and reliable network of representatives and agents.

Through them, Livingstone organised a demonstration for Einar Petersen, a Swedish Golf Federation expert—again targeting an industry opinion leader. The demonstration went well, despite some minor hitches, which did not faze Livingstone: 'Always you get something going wrong. Murphy's Law prevails under these circumstances, but the main thing is to stay cool, be confident . . . and use it as a training session for the people around you because, if we get it wrong, they're certainly going to get it wrong.' Petersen is positive: 'I'm very impressed. It's a machine I've been seeing overseas in England and the States and I read about it in the magazines, but it's very good to see in Swedish ground now.'

Livingstone's hands-on involvement is a key element of his marketing. He stresses the importance of personal contact, particularly on the first approach to a new market or major customer. 'People see brochures, they see facsimiles, and they really don't know what to expect,' he says. 'They've probably never seen the machine before, they've certainly never seen you before and the first impressions really count. I've always made it a policy that I personally go in and do the set-up, negotiate the contracts and try . . . to win their confidence. We usually give a complete demonstration of everything that could possibly go right and wrong with our machinery on the course and then follow through with another meeting.'

He thinks that his presence as managing director of his company encourages potential customers to take his demonstrations seriously: 'It's not uncommon for people not only to have their key people from their own organisation on site but they also call in industry experts, consultants . . . and, if you get past the independent contractors or experts and the managing directors of the companies, you've got a deal on your hands.'

Livingstone took personal involvement to extraordinary lengths in another important market, Japan, where he has been selling his machines since 1987. When he introduced a new gearbox for the Coremaster, a machine sold to Japan developed an oil-seal leak. 'The last thing anybody wants on a putting green is oil dripping down,' he says. Livingstone was in Sydney but, as soon as he heard of the problem, got the necessary components and left on a Tokyo-bound plane the same day. He arrived early the next morning, went straight to the golf course and fixed the leak. 'That blew the Japanese impression of Australians being slack,' he says. The lesson: 'You must look after your product credibility.'

Livingstone's marketing methods are working. His annual turnover from export topped $5 million in 1989 and Coremaster has 'become a cult figure'. He is readying a new generation of the machine and an expanding range of ancillary equipment. While sales in Europe and Asia are important, he expects his biggest growth to occur in the United States. And he sees opportunities beyond commercial turf applications: 'Americans are very houseproud and particularly the wealthy people want to have their lawns manicured, and there's a whole new market which we could very easily penetrate simply by adapting our technology, scaling down the size of the machines, so that they could be used in domestic situations.'

David Livingstone waves no national flags when he markets Coremaster overseas. Indeed, many of his customers do not realise that his machinery is Australian until they have met him or done a deal with his company. But, for some

Australian exporters, their home country—and its image and mythology—have constituted the central plank in their international marketing strategies.

Two such marketers are John Chatham, of Beecham Beverages, and Colin Dangaard, of Australian Stock Saddles. Their products are very different: mineral water flavoured with fruit juice for Chatham and Australian bush gear, particularly saddles, for Dangaard. And their personal styles are even more divergent: Chatham is a quietly spoken, meticulous, marketing man's marketing man; Dangaard is a boisterous extrovert and a natural salesman. While Chatham spends much of his time in interviews being careful not to give away too much of interest to his competitors, Dangaard declares cheerfully about his success in the United States: 'I came here on a mission of plunder in the first place. I thought, well, I'm gonna rip them off for as much money as I can and plunder their women, take their money and have a lot of fun, and finally I'm managing to do it.'

Where there is no difference between them is in playing up the Australian origins of their products. One of the national cliches of our time is that Australia is 'flavour of the month' in North America. The phrase suggests a fad, a brief, inevitably fickle, dalliance. What belies that is that the cliche has now been around for a lot of months—most of the last decade, in fact. Both Chatham and Dangaard have taken advantage of the phenomenon it describes for at least several years and believe it has much more life in it yet.

Chatham: 'We're selling Australia. That's a very good image to have [in the United States] at the moment and . . . it'll probably continue for some time because there's tremendous interest in Australia and in Australians in general. So the image works very well for us.'

Dangaard: 'A lot of Australians get nervous. They say, "We can't keep producing like this; it makes me really nervous, selling more and more". I say, no, no, keep selling. They say, "The market's going to flatten out". No, it's not. Americans are buying more and more of Australia. They're totally fascinated by us, and particularly by our style of riding and the legend of the Man from the Snowy River, the bush.

So you keep makin' 'em. I'll keep sellin' 'em.'

Chatham says the nationalist image not only works in the United States: 'It's just as strong, if not stronger, in Canada and it's very strong in Japan . . . Australia is seen as a bit like the last frontier. It's out of the way of a lot of the pollution and the nuclear problems of the northern hemisphere. It's seen as somewhere people can still go and feel as though they've got back to nature . . . In Europe even, our image is also stronger than I thought it was and certainly quite positive in places like Germany and the UK.'

Mineral water flavoured with natural fruit juice was launched on the Australian market under the Deep Spring label in 1980. Beecham Beverages took it over in 1983. Orange, mango, lemon, lime, passionfruit, apple, kiwi fruit, blackcurrant, grapefruit and mandarin were used in various combinations to provide the flavours. It took only five years for the mixes to grab 15 per cent of Australian soft-drink sales—a major marketing success, given the competition it faced from the Cokes and Pepsis of this world.

With that success, Beecham Beverages decided a good opportunity existed in North America. The mineral water–fruit juice mix was unknown there. Although he is a firm believer in market research, managing director, John Chatham, admits that there was limited analysis done before the decision was made to take the drink into the US. The time and the product felt right.

The rest of the marketing was very carefully handled. The first big decision was the naming of the product. It was given a new name for North America: Koala Springs. The name has now been shortened simply to Koala. 'Koala itself is a good name and a good image to have because it says Australia without actually having anything more complicated and it's a very simple word,' says Chatham. 'The brand itself did give us a unique positioning . . . We've got such a good image to work with, we can use that image to create a feeling of warmth and friendliness and a very positive emotional response to the product.'

Considerable effort went into advertising. Beecham television commercials promote the koala humorously but work very hard at pushing the 'natural' aspect of the product

'We've certainly put a lot of money into advertising, probably more than most people in this sector—or in this bottled-water market, as it's called in America,' he says. The advertising is directed at both the trade and general consumers.

Concentrating initially on California, Beecham succeeded with its launch. From zero sales in April 1986, it was selling 100 000 cases a month by September. Given that it is essentially a very simple, unpatentable product, it was only a matter of time before it had rivals, not only from with the United States but also from Australia. Chatham has worked very hard at all aspects of marketing to ward off the challengers. He has succeeded. In 1989, North American retail sales were approaching $US200 million and Koala had established itself as the leading brand in its sector of the soft-drink market.

He has built up a strong distribution system, particularly on the West Coast but now stretching across the United States and into Canada. He tries to avoid distributors who handle other soft drinks so that there can be no question of divided loyalties. He has warehousing facilities in San Francisco to make sure that any shipping delays do not interfere with the flow of his product into the market. He personally worries about details in the marketing chain such as the placement of his drinks in supermarkets.

He has also developed with designers in Melbourne a range of products to promote his drink—T-shirts, sweat-shirts, sun visors, sports bags, baseball caps and umbrellas. All feature a koala logo as well as the brand name. So successful have these gimmicks been that they have become marketable commodities in their own right. According to Chatham, they create 'a very good, warm, friendly image with the children and the adults as well'. 'That's a key part of our marketing program. It's as important as getting out there and actually selling the product because, by creating that warm feeling towards us, we're creating a good attitude towards the product. People relate well to it and that's as good as advertising.

'It's okay to go out and advertise . . . It's okay to actually get the product on the shelf but you lose a lot of your opportunity if you don't capitalise on things like the image and the emotional responses that you can create around the brand. And point-of-sale material and what we call novelty products, which are the T-shirts and the baseball hats—all these sorts of things extend the brand into an extra dimension.'

The cartoon koalas in promotional products and television commercials cloak a serious marketing purpose. They contribute to the image Chatham seeks: 'When people look at Koala Springs, they just don't look at something in a bottle. They actually look at something that means Australia, fun, irreverence, let's have fun. It's associated with party situations or with a good time over dinner or having a good time at the beach.'

Despite his belief in the benefits of Australia's image in North America, Chatham cautions against undue reliance on it: 'I don't think it will sell the product for you if the product's no good . . . You've got to have a product that stands up for itself.'

This lesson is even more pertinent in Asia. Koala Springs is already selling in Singapore and, in 1989, Chatham was preparing to enter the Japanese market. 'When you start tackling the Asian markets, you really have to start thinking more about researching the product before you go into them, because the whole concept of Australia—even the fact that Australia exists—in some places isn't all that clear.' He has found, for example, that the koala is a good image for Japan, where the animal has been a popular object of curiosity. But, when Taiwanese were asked what animal they associated with Australia, they did not go for koalas or kangaroos or the like; the majority replied: 'cows'. Not an exciting result for the Koala Springs image-makers.

In Asia, Chatham is putting considerable effort into market research. This is not just to test advertising slogans. More basically, it is to prepare his product: 'Certain markets have different taste profiles, so you have to look at adjusting a product that is dependent on taste, as our product is, . . . to suit the conditions of [a particular] market . . . We're prepared to make the product what the market wants. It's no good going in there and saying, "Hey, we've got this wonderful product", and throwing it at the market and expecting people to drink it. That's not the way to do it.'

Colin Dangaard knows that, too. He saw an opening for Australian stock saddles in the unlikeliest place—the American West. But they had to be adjusted to the market. American horses, their frames rooted in the heavy quarterhorse, are wider and bigger than thinner, more thoroughbred Australian types. Unchanged, Australian stock saddles would not have fitted most American horses. Or their riders, as the backsides of humans also vary.

So he accommodated those variations. The part of a saddle that fits over the spine of a horse is called the 'chamber'; Dangaard's most popular saddle comes in four different sizes of chamber so that it can fit just about any horse in the United States. And it has 10 different seat sizes so that it suits just about any American rider. In addition, Dangaard ensures his saddles have other non-Australian features, such as roping horns and fancy tooling, if his American customers want them.

Dangaard recognised a potential North American niche for the Australian saddles back in the late 1970s. He was living in Los Angeles where he wrote a successful syndicated show-business column—hardly a conventional background for an expert on saddles. But Dangaard was reared in Mareeba, in the far north of Queensland, and knew about horses and related matters. Throughout his career as a journalist, he had not lost his interest in them.

There were several reasons for the US opportunity. Americans were used to the Western saddle, which is much bigger and heavier than its Australian counterpart; its size and a horn on the front made it ideal for roping cattle. But that function is irrelevant for recreational riders. And the weight is a problem for women—and 70 per cent of the eight million Americans who ride horses are female. In contrast, the small, light Australian stock saddle is easy to handle. Many Americans also have to go into mountain areas to ride, as housing developments have gobbled up the flat land. And here the Australian stock saddle has a big advantage: it has knee-pads which help the rider hold his seat in the steepest terrain.

Whatever the reasons, the opportunity might have remained unrealised had it not been for two vital factors: the Australian movie *The Man from Snowy River* and Dangaard's exuberant, personalised—and very nationalistic—marketing. Released in 1982, the film did very strong business in North America. To Dangaard, it was almost like a feature-length commercial: with its stunning images of horsemen charging down almost perpendicular slopes, nothing could have shown off the advantages of the Australian stock saddle more effectively.

The connection still works. He describes the aftermath of some of his US sales: 'They call me up two months later and say, "I did it. I rode like the Man from Snowy River. I came down a mountain." I go, oh, no. Her people are going to be talking to my people, if she keeps this up.'

Dangaard gave away journalism in the mid-1980s to devote himself full-time to his company, Australian Stock Saddles. Now married to an American who is also his partner, he lives on a ranch at Malibu, just outside Los Angeles, and runs his business from there. But he spends a lot of time travelling to horse and mule shows around America. He sells saddles and other Australian gear, such as hats and whips, at the shows. And he is a 'natural' at the patter and hustle of a salesman.

The shows serve a longer-term purpose of establishing his ongoing presence in the market. That presence is distinctively Australian. From his bush hat to the 'G'day' in his greetings, he milks his home country's image for all it is worth.

Dangaard has also been able to benefit from his background in show-business journalism. Some of his contacts from those days have become customers and friends and his saddles are used by the likes of Bo Derek, Robert Wagner, Patrick Swayze and William Shatner. In the specialist magazines which service the horse riders of America, photographs of them atop a stock saddle help Dangaard establish a marketable profile. Although he is not a friend, there is another former film actor who has one of his saddles: Ronald Reagan.

Dangaard now sells about $US2 million worth of saddle

and other bush gear in the United States each year. He has got his saddles from several Australian manufacturers but the biggest seller—the Somerset—comes from Trevor James, whose staff make them by hand at a saddlery in the Brisbane suburb of Lawnton. James sells about five saddles a day in the United States through Dangaard. At $US900–$1500 per saddle, that's a good return for a small business. James is now exploring the possibility of selling his saddles into Italy and Singapore. But he admits that it would help if there were Italian and Singaporean equivalents of Colin Dangaard to do his marketing for him.

In their different ways, Argyle Diamonds, David Livingstone, John Chatham and Colin Dangaard have found niches for their products in overseas markets. All have positioned themselves prominently in those markets: Argyle through its pink diamond auctions and its 'champagne and cognac' campaigns; Livingstone through selling to the world's top sporting turf locations; Chatham through being first into the North American market and then using heavy advertising and promotion that take advantage Australia's strong image in the United States; Dangaard through pushing the same nationalist message with good old-fashioned hustle and a handy association with Hollywood celebrities.

All of them study their markets carefully. Argyle has had to deal with a very complex market, with entrenched selling arrangements but with new opportunities opening up, particularly with less expensive diamond jewellery. Livingstone has put a lot of personal effort and travel into getting to know his markets and, in addition, has taken good advantage of AUSTRADE help him understand them. Chatham has a strong commitment to market research, both to sustain Koala Springs' market edge in North America and to prepare its launch into new Asian markets. Dangaard, whose carefree manner does not obscure a shrewd business brain, gets continual feedback on his market through frequent travel to horse and mule shows.

Where appropriate, trade shows and similar opportunities have been important. Livingstone goes to three a year and Dangaard has his regular events. Argyle demonstrated new cutting and polishing technology at Surat in India and, in a sense, its Christie's New York auction was an occasion for display.

Chatham and Dangaard have also adjusted their products to meet the needs of their markets. Livingstone is adding new elements to his Coremaster aerator to increase its attractiveness to buyers; and he is looking at major variations in size to reach into an entirely new, American domestic market. Argyle is directly intervening in the processing of its product to reach into an important market by its encouragement of new cutting and polishing equipment in India.

What all them demonstrate is that good products need good marketing. It is only then that their export potential will be realised.

4 The Managers

MANY Australian manufacturers face barriers to export within themselves. They lack experience of it. They are often frightened of it. Or, dulled by decades of protection, they think only of their domestic market. If the domestic market is strong, why take on the risks and hassles of going into strange foreign markets? If the domestic market is weak, why not reduce the workforce and cut other costs to try to maintain profitability, instead of seeking growth overseas?

Surveying Australians' lack of export aggressiveness in mid-1989, Senator John Button, as the responsible Minister in the Hawke Government, observed:

> I think the companies by and large which have the global view have been forced into having [it]. That is, . . . they've grown up here in this environment, become very successful in Australia, [but] the Australian market is too small. So they go overseas. That's very sensible. Others have gone overseas because they have a technology, perhaps a very good technology; bu t . . . again the Australian market is too small. So they say, this technology has worldwide applications, so the world becomes our market.
>
> There are plenty of others who could do that and who don't, and a lot of it . . . has to do with inadequate management, a lack of vision . . . I don't think it's fair to blame people for that. Much of that is the legacy from the past . . .
>
> In the world debate about industry policy, one of the recognised advantages of the Japanese against the Americans, against many of the Europeans and against us, is that they look ahead ten years; they say, 'Where is this company going to be in ten years' time?' Now, I think if a lot of Australian chief executives asked themselves that question honestly, they would go white.

A relative newcomer to the commercial world, Dr Ben Greene, whose high-tech activities were described in chapter 2, has quickly formed the iconoclastic view that Australian management attitudes are a barrier to export. 'I just think that they're outdated,' he says. 'They are derived in an experience and a corporate history in Australia which is becoming irrelevant as we speak. I think that the ethos of international competition is given a lot of lip service in boardrooms right round this country but the commitment of real capital and real resources to get there and break in just isn't there.'

There is no simple formula for Australian managers to apply to enable them to succeed in export. Export is like management itself: an imprecise art.

Not that all managers have always thought that what they did had to be so imprecise. During the 1970s and early 1980s as a wave of management consciousness swept Australia some managers went out in search of a holy grail Management consultancies abounded, business schools expanded and management texts suddenly became best sellers to help them find it. 'It' was 'the model' which would tell them how to become better managers and how to get better results for their companies.

Books like *In Search of Excelllence* by Tom Peters and Robert H. Waterman and *The Change Masters* by Elizabeth Moss Kanter became the bibles of some executives understanding and adapting their theories to particular environments the mark of the blessed disciple. Much management theory revolved around simple ideas which if applied in the kind of stabilised environment artificially postulated by management consultants, provided 'the model' to follow.

It could never be so simple. Companies are dynamic organisms made up of numerous changing cells. And simple model for universal change will almost never succeed Tom Peters now writes about 'managing chaos'.

And so it is with export. John Hemphill, AUSTRADE' Communications Manager, has seen a lot of managers succeed and fail in export. To him, the essential ingredient for those who succeed apply to all aspects of management 'flexibility and responsiveness, together with internal capability, financial resilience and stamina'.

Managers need to plan for the unplannable. They need to have a clear direction or vision of where they're going but not be overcommitted as to how they are going to get there. Their thinking must be strategic in focus, yet they must be flexible and responsive to changes in the market. To achieve this, they must be more knowledgeable than ever before—not only about their competition, but also about their own capability.

If we are going to compete effectively in the global market, our managers, our leaders in industry, must maximise capability by matching their companies' technical systems to their people resources. The successful managers will be those who are responsive to changes in the market and changes in the workplace.

Strategically, they must be thinking about how and where and when to position themselves in the value-added chain. Quality is perhaps the key issue—quality of information about competitors, quality and clarity of objectives, quality of their financial resilience and quality of the people who will make it happen.

In this chapter, we look at four Australian company heads who have shown the necessary qualities to make it in export. None of them has a Harvard MBA but all have been skilful in their creation and exploitation of international opportunities.

The first is Finnish-born Heimo Eberhardt, who manufactures scientific equipment and computers in Melbourne. He has taken his company into Western Europe, the United States and Asia. But, above all, he is better positioned than any other Australian manufacturer to exploit the new export opportunities opening up in the USSR and Eastern Europe.

Next is Frank Bannigan who has developed the manufacture of everyday household electrical appliances into an international business. His company, Kambrook, is small compared to some of its multinational rivals. But he has turned this to his advantage by exploiting consumer trends with a speed his opponents cannot match.

Then there is Maggie Shepherd who started making clothes for friends from her home in Canberra and who now runs a chain of stores in Australia and the United States.

Finally, there is Frank Seeley, who makes evaporative air conditioners in Adelaide. Once, he didn't want to know about export. He did not need it, he thought. Now, Seeley International is the world leader in sales of its kind of products.

Heimo Eberhardt is not the kind of chief executive who leads from behind. Exports account for more than 80 per cent of the sales of his company, Labtam Limited. But Eberhardt does not direct this international marketing effort from a desk in his Melbourne head office, with occasional forays overseas. Instead, he travels the world for about eight months a year.

It has had its costs: not enough time with his kids, a regretted involvement with a management investment company and a marriage separation. It has also had its rewards: a rapidly growing scientific instrument and computer company selling into Asia, Europe and the United States. And he is increasingly concentrating much of his energy on establishing a permanent presence in one of the most fascinating markets in the world—Eastern Europe. Boyish-faced and in his early forties, Eberhardt gets his biggest kicks from doing business wherever it takes him.

Eberhardt, who studied engineering at the Royal Melbourne Institute of Technology, began his entrepreneurial career in 1972. He set up a company in partnership with Don Dryden, with whom he had worked at the multinational Philips organisation. Through the company, R & D Instruments Pty Ltd, they sold equipment brought in from overseas. That its orientation was towards importing, rather than exporting, reflected the attitudes of the time. Although the partners had manufacturing ambitions even then, when they discussed their ideas with their bank manager, Eberhardt remembers that he discouraged them by declaring: 'Australia's no place to have a manufacturing company. You're crazy. You should be an import company.' His advice prevailed, at least for a few years, but formed, at the same time, a kind of challenge.

'That statement haunted me for years,' Eberhardt says

'I just didn't believe it and, because of that, it made me probably more determined to prove that people are wrong. Things can be done if you have the will and foresight and stubbornness for staying there and hanging on. I'm not a quitter.'

R & D Instruments at first had sufficient funds to pay rent, telephone bills and basic overheads 'but not enough money to pay salaries or anything like that', Eberhardt remembers. The firm could not even afford air or train fares so that, if Eberhardt needed to go interstate, he would drive his own Ford Falcon there, sleep in the back seat, make his selling rounds in it and then drive back to Melbourne.

Despite these difficulties and his concentration on imports, Eberhardt was able to develop strong export skills and awareness in those early years. This was because of a consultancy to an American company which took him throughout Asia where he demonstrated, sold, installed, and trained operators for US equipment.

After a period of 'trying to make a dollar on anything we could' as Eberhardt puts it, he and Dryden began to specialise in the importation and sales of emission spectrometer systems. These are used to analyse the elements in substances. They have uses for analysing elements in ore in the mining industry; in soil in agriculture; medical uses; and so on. They formed Labtest Equipment Co. (S. E. Asia) Pty Ltd to operate in this area. Eventually, R & D Instruments and Labtest Equipment were combined into one company—Labtam.

The growing specialisation led inexorably to the manufacture of their own products. At an international conference at Melbourne's Monash University in 1975, Eberhardt and Dryden learned of a new analytical technique using an emission source known as inductively coupled plasma (ICP). Combined with suitable optical equipment, ICP was a big step forward in elemental analysis. Eberhardt and Dryden quickly embarked on a research and development program to develop their own spectrometer using ICP. They were joined at this time by David Tam and Trevor Knight and together they developed the forerunner of a family of spectrometers known as 'Plasmascan'.

Eberhardt's knowledge of the market, gained during his consultancy for Americans, now came into play. He took Plasmascan overseas and won orders in South-East Asia, Europe, South Africa and India.

'If I'd stayed in Australia in an office, I think that Labtam would not be where it is,' Eberhardt says. 'The most important function for me is to know what the market wants and then, reflecting that back, what we have to design, develop and manufacture. I'm very sensitive to quality and customer satisfaction. I'm very sensitive [to the need] that we deliver the type of products the customers are asking for and the quickest way this can occur is that I personally find out and personally talk to the customers . . .

'Always when I go into a market, I find key people in this market and I get to know them and they get to know me. From those key people I find out where and how I can approach the market, because every market is different.'

Reflecting Eberhardt's emphasis on meeting customers' needs, Labtam has continually emphasised research and development activities. Dryden estimates that the company spends about 12 per cent of its annual turnover on R & D. This has not only kept it at the cutting edge of spectrometry but has opened up a major involvement in computers and information systems. That happened after the development of Plasmascan, when it became apparent that a more powerful computer was needed to process the information generated by the spectrometers. David Tam convinced his associates that he could design and develop a Labtam computer. The result was the Labtam Series 3000 computers which were first installed commercially in 1983. Improved computers and spectrometers have followed.

Throughout this period, Eberhardt kept looking for new markets. The company's overseas representation now includes an office in West Germany and direct distributors in North and South-East Asia, the United Arab Emirates, Chile, New Zealand and South Africa.

An otherwise unhappy experience for him led to one major foreign advance. In the mid-1980s, Labtam was restructured so that it came under the effective control of a management investment company (MIC). Eberhardt, who retained 49 per cent of the shares, thought this would provide needed management support for the company's expanding activities which took him away from Australia so often. But, he says, he was increasingly shut out of its operations. When he was in Melbourne, he stopped going to the office and, instead, worked from home. Above all, he threw himself into overseas marketing, including in India. The result was the formation of a joint venture company on the subcontinent. Called Datalab, it is 60 per cent owned by Indian investors and 40 per cent by Labtam. It cost Labtam about $2 million to get the new company and its manufacturing operations going but in one contract alone in mid-1989 it secured sales in India of $3.5 million. (In the meantime, in 1987 he borrowed overseas so that he could buy out the MIC and establish his sovereignty over Labtam. 'All MICs do is add to your overheads,' he now says dismissively.)

One overseas development has overshadowed all others in the 1980s—the move by Eberhardt and Labtam into Eastern Europe. It began with his first visit to the USSR at the end of 1979 and involved a degree of luck and intelligent opportunism. Since then, a lot of time, money and effort have gone into capitalising on that promising beginning. He has made sales to Hungary and Romania and is looking closely at Poland's potential. But the USSR remains the primary target.

On his first visit there, he took with him a spectrometer which contained some new and unusual Labtam technology to display at a technical exhibition. After repeated inspections of his equipment, two Soviet scientists invited him to an institute run by the Geology Ministry. There they had installed some French spectrometers, similar to his, but an engineer had spent a year trying—without success—to make them work. Eberhardt spotted the problem and was able to use parts for his own spectrometer to make the French equipment function.

The Russians' gratitude led to a delegation going to Melbourne to inspected Labtam's products. Soviet orders followed, slowly at first but then gaining momentum. 'It took four years before the orders really started to roll in and we started to make a real profit,' Eberhardt says.

Returns have to be high to cover the costs of trading with the USSR. 'Moscow is the most expensive place in the world to do business,' Eberhardt says bluntly. He has an office and apartment in the World Trade Centre, a hotel, business and apartment complex on the banks of the Moscow River. The office is, in fact, a converted apartment—with the conversion carried out by Finnish builders, nominated by Soviet authorities, at an extraordinary cost of $A750 000 (of which the government would have received around half).

Agustin Gomez de Sergura, a multilingual Soviet citizen who is the son of a Spanish communist who fled from Franco to Russia, is the permanent head of the office. Victoria Grekova, an English-speaking Russian, is executive assistant. As his own Russian is limited, Eberhardt needs the fluency of his local aides. But their importance goes beyond that. In a capital city which has neither a telephone directory nor street maps and in which contacts count, their input is vital.

Eberhardt estimates Labtam's annual overheads in Moscow at around $A2 million a year. He says that image, generally very important in the USSR, was particularly important to Labtam, which wanted to be seen as progressive and technological and from a country which is 'more than sheep and wheat and wool'. In addition, he stresses the advantages of a permanent presence: 'You have to be here. People are not interested in having to call Australia. Even a telex has to be approved by a vice-minister.'

He has kept up a high level of financial commitment even though Soviet trade has declined recently. 'Last year [1988], sales were one quarter of what they were the year before and the year before they were half what they were the year before that,' he says. But, entering 1990, he was looking forward to the introduction of the first five-year plan to be devised under Mikhail Gorbachev. He is aiming for a massive increase in annual turnover—to around $100 million—in the next few years.

At the same time, Eberhardt warns against seeing the USSR as a land of easy pickings. It is not. 'Because of the political climate,' he says, 'this country is the romantic country and everybody wants to be involved in Russia. Everybody want-to do business here. It is a huge market and there's nothing they don't need so the potential is absolutely enormous . . . [But] this market has no overnight successes. Anybody who wants to come in here has to be in for the long haul and do it right. This market's a very demanding market for quality, product, price—very demanding and, if you don't do it right and you're not in there for the long haul, you'll fail . . . It's something that people dream of—rolling in, signing big contracts and rolling out. It really doesn't happen like that.'

He points out that the USSR has also become a more complicated place in which to do business. Until perestroika, imported goods were generally purchased by large centralised government organisations for the entire Soviet Union. Now, purchasing decisions are being decentralised down to factory level. 'The people who are the end users have to justify what they buy and they have to make things work . . . be productive.' In addition, hard currency shortages mean that the Soviets are very selective about what they buy.

Eberhardt's way of dealing with the changes is to go into joint ventures with Soviet instrumentalities. He estimates Labtam spent about $A5 million in 1988–89 setting up several joint venture companies in Moscow. He says that the Soviet Government has been encouraging joint ventures in recent years but most have been with engineering companies. His joint ventures are among the first in the high-tech field.

About $A3 million of Labtam's joint-venture set-up costs have gone into one company, ASTEC (Australian Soviet Technology), which is 51 per cent owned by the Soviet Ministry of Health and 49 per cent by Labtam. Its first task is to manufacture a device for analysing blood flowing into the heart as a means of anticipating cardiac problems. It is the result of research at a Ministry of Health cardiology centre in Moscow into predicting—and thereby preventing—heart attacks, in preference to a more Western-style concentration on curative techniques. The Soviet scientists at the cardiology centre have patented some of the processes to be contained in the device and these will be combined with Labtam technology. Labtam will make the circuit boards for the devices in Australia and will provide design, marketing and other expertise. Otherwise, the instruments will be manufactured in Russia.

Eberhardt sees a huge market for the devices in the USSR alone. Importantly for Soviet authorities hungry for hard currency, he believes that there are very large potential sales in the West, where the devices should have a technological edge. But he already sees a need for diversification: 'This is the first product. There will have to be more to have a successful company.'

For staff, ASTEC will take over the employment of scientists and technicians currently on the payroll of the Ministry of Health. This will generally mean higher salaries and, for some, the prized perk of travel outside the USSR. For his part, Eberhardt praises the dedication of the locals, citing examples of people sleeping beside their computers so they could give the maximum time to urgent projects.

Australian manufacturers have not been quick to take advantage of the new commercial opportunities opening up in the USSR and elsewhere in Eastern Europe. In 1989, only two Australian companies, other than Labtam, had full accreditation to trade with the Russians and thus have permanent offices and other privileges. One was the Elders group, which has a long history of selling primary products there, and the other a small general trading operation. So, for manufacturing industry, Eberhardt has shown the way. And he has gone a lot further than accreditation: he has built the company infrastructure which will maximise his chances for growth. Provided the Soviet Union does not suddenly reverse its new policies of openness to the West, he is in the box seat.

In the beginning, Frank Bannigan was like a corporal with a field marshal's baton in his knapsack. He started his working life as an electrician. He did an apprenticeship and qualified as a tradesman in the mineral city of Broken Hill in the far west of New South Wales. He then worked at his trade in Sydney and Canberra before settling in Melbourne in the early 1960s. Throughout this period, he had loftier aims. 'It was always my ambition to have a factory as distinct from working at doing electrical installations, he says. With this as his ultimate goal, he founded the Kambrook company in 1964—in the garage of his suburban Melbourne home. But he was to get the factory of his dreams with remarkable speed.

Kambrook was initially simply an electrical contracting company. Through the late 1960s, Bannigan picked up a series of contracts to put in wiring for refrigeration equipment in suburban Melbourne supermarkets. Frozen foods were taking off in a big way in Australia and, with them, there was a boom in supermarket refrigeration. In carrying out his work, Bannigan encountered a common problem: the refrigeration control equipment required an inordinate number of power points. So he designed a plastic panel into which the wiring for a number of pieces of equipment could be fed; the panel could then be plugged into a single power point which thus could supply multiple electrical needs.

Bannigan began making the panels for use with refrigeration equipment and, at $300-$400 each, it was a tidy sideline to his contracting work. But he did not stop there. 'We thought there must be another way of using this panel,' he says. 'So I came up with the idea of putting four power points on the panel.'

Bannigan quickly recognised that the 'power board' as he called it, would have much wider uses than refrigeration. At the time, Australian houses commonly had very few power points—one point per room and sometimes not even that. Yet Australian society was seeing a rapid proliferation of electrical household appliances. Double adapters were joined to double adapters and then plugged into those few power points to enable the simultaneous use of these appliances: blenders, toasters, jugs, cookware and other kitchen equipment; televisions, heaters, stereos and lamps in living rooms; electric blankets, hair driers, even electric guitars in bedrooms. They were powered through little trees of adapters growing horizontally out of skirting boards. The power board was to end all that.

He got only what he remembers as an uninquisitive stunned reaction' from the first retail buyers to see his invention. He got a better response, however, from the buyers for the K-Mart chain. They were interested. This time the shortcomings were Bannigan's. They wanted to know about prices, trading terms, packaging and the like and Bannigan had not thought about them. They suggested he go away and work out a proposal. A week later, he returned with a detailed proposition and it took only another week before K-Mart gave him his first order—for 250 power boards. They sold out almost immediately. Kambrook, despite an inadequate infrastructure, was on its way.

Bannigan made the first power boards for K-Mart in a workshop at the back of a shop which housed his contracting business in 1970. Now, he has a factory covering 25 000 square metres and employing 600 people. It produces about 30 000 individual products every day and the range is extensive: appliances include coffee makers, toasters, steam irons, food and water heaters, juicers, can openers, timers, heaters, electrical barbecues, personal care items and garden lighting. An estimated 85 per cent of Australian homes have at least one of those products. So do a lot of householders in 28 other countries. For, as he has moved into the global market, Bannigan has learned and applied some valuable lessons.

First, in the fiercely competitive electrical goods market, dominated by multinationals, he puts strong emphasis on continually coming up with new products. Kambrook spends about $4 million a year on research and development. It also works hard at projecting an innovative image. With its heavy advertising budget, Bannigan says, 'we only advertise products that are different and unique—products that we've invented ourselves. We don't want to advertise products that everyone else has, like toasters.'

The second lesson is to stick to making household appliances which are truly useful. 'They are the products that we use every day of the week,' Bannigan says. 'They're not just gimmicks . . . Times haven't exactly been easy in the last few years but when you've got core products that are useful products, people will always buy them because they need them. So that's been one of the fundamental qualities of the company right since conception.' From cordless irons to smokeless grills, Kambrook product frequently involve a familiar household item with an innovative advantage.

Design figures prominently in his reckoning. 'Design is everything,' he says. 'If you are serious about the global market, then you have to be serious about your design. You look at any of the Kambrook products. The work that goes into designing them—not for the Australian market only but for the global market—is quite an exercise.'

Bannigan's concern with design extends to the packaging of his products. Kambrook sticks to bold packaging in full colour so that its products stand out on store shelves. But, to Bannigan, design is not just how to make things look attractive or striking. It is also how to incorporate the best features at the least cost—'It's no good designing something which will ultimately cost more than our consumer can pay for it'—and to make sure that those features are what the market, in its various guises, wants.

He keeps a close eye on a process which, for each new product, begins with in-house designers spending two or three weeks making many drawings to test colour and shape concepts. The favoured design will then be tested by making a model in timber or some other material. The manufacturing implications of the design will be kept in focus at all times. At the end of the process should be a product which will appeal to all, not just some, of the markets in which it will be sold.

'I think what a lot of people are doing is trying to sell their Australian ideas and design without actually going overseas and looking at the markets,' he says. He points to severely practical reasons for familiarity with overseas markets: his products must meet electrical and safety standards and these must therefore be incorporated in products at the design stage. Other products often run up against regulatory standards. The answer, he argues, is to know about these in advance so that a manufacturer can come up with a 'universal design' which caters for all markets.

Knowing about the requirements of overseas markets at the design stage has cost benefits. 'Designing products for the world market means that our cost of design here is spread over a lot more units at the end of the day,' he says. It also means that the company gets value for its expenditure on tooling.

In exploiting overseas markets, Bannigan recognises his weaknesses and concentrates on his strengths. He does not try to sell toasters in the USA, for example: 'They seem to buy a toaster which doesn't have the features that we need for our market. They don't paint the underside of the toaster, they use different gauge metals and things that we can't get away with in Australia.' So Kambrook toasters are designed with only the European and Australian markets in mind.

On the other hand, Kambrook is now designing telephones which can be made in Australia more cheaply than the cost of buying them in Taiwan or China. 'The reason we can do that is the design of the circuits,' he says. Holding up a circuit board, which is not much broader and a lot slimmer than the palm of his hand, he adds: 'This circuit is completely designed and made in Australia.' This one part is the functional part of the telephone—the rest is packaging— whereas a normal telephone could have three or four similar components wired or soldered together. The size and simplicity of the circuit board in turn makes the task of fitting it into a casing much less complicated and therefore much less expensive. The result: 'We have a product which is going to be very competitive on a global scale.'

Bannigan has developed the flexibility to move quickly into the market so that his appliances can become established before the much bigger multinationals can swamp them with rival products. He has also developed considerable flexibility in his methods of getting his products made. For the Australian market, Kambrook's Goldstar division imports televisions, video recorders and players, tape recorders, audio systems and personal computers from Korea. Some components for other Kambrook products are also imported. For export, Kambrook manufactures in New Zealand, as well as Australia, although Bannigan's favoured method of getting into foreign markets is through licensing the manufacture of his products by overseas companies Currently, they are made under licence in the UK and China

It took him a few years to get it right in the UK. He had a number of different agents and distributors and then tried a joint manufacturing venture in Ireland with mixed results. Although he was convinced that 'we can't make product in Australia and export it to the UK,' he did not find the solution until he went into a licensing arrangement with a young English company with the decidely un-English name of Cordon Bleu. Cordon Bleu, which manufactures at King's Lynn in Norfolk, was a competitor in the sense that it was already in the electrical-goods industry. 'By being in the electrical industry, they know the retailers, they know the buyers, they know the market exceptionally well,' Bannigan says. 'So we've established that by working with people who know the market, we have a better opportunity getting our products distributed here.'

Richard Preece, the Chairman of Cordon Bleu, says of the arrangement: 'I knew that Kambrook were getting into the UK market with another Australian company who had a factory in Ireland and I knew that Frank felt that it wasn't an entirely satisfactory way of attacking the British market . . . [The other] Australian company were geared up into another market sector and, although there appeared to be a synergy between the businesses, because they were in different products and because the factory that was producing the merchandise was offshore, it didn't actually work out 100 per cent . . . So I suggested to him that we get together and we started running their product from the beginning of 1987 and things have really gone forward from that point. We've had tremendous increases in sales and penetration of the market. It's been very successful for both companies.

'I think the most important thing in getting into any new market is to go and observe the market, meet the people, learn who the brands are in the market, why they're successful at selling and take it from there,' Preece says. 'Then you've got to constantly update yourself on the position in the market, visit it constantly, have your own people in it, and be prepared to adapt your technique to the particular market . . . I think it's far better, if you're not sure of the right way to attack a market, perhaps to pick a partner in that country in the same way that we of Cordon Bleu and Kambrook work together in partnership.'

Kambrook now devises the designs and makes components and tooling in Australia and ships them to Cordon Bleu where they are transformed into products which, while bearing the Kambrook label, are marketed in packages which bear a Union Jack and a 'Made in England' slogan. Preece says it is important to give the products a UK identity, while Bannigan shrugs and comments: 'If it sells products, that's what it's about, isn't it?' What matters to him is that, for every Kambrook product running down the production line in the Cordon Bleu factory, there is a royalty going back to Australia.

According to Bannigan, Cordon Bleu has been able to get Kambrook products into virtually every shopping centre in the UK. In 1989, at a time when many British electrical goods factories are working only two-day weeks because of a downturn in consumer spending, Cordon Bleu was operating full-time. The power board had been the backbone of the licensing arrangement but the UK company then launched a much wider range of Kambrook appliances.

There is a long-term benefit in the arrangement for Kambrook. With the dropping of tariff barriers within a united Europe in 1992, many non-European companies are worried about access to this rich market. His partnership with Cordon Bleu has given Bannigan a foothold in that market. He has also negotiated a deal with a Spanish electrical company for the supply of components which he will manufacture under licence in China.

Until 1989, manufacturing under licence in China's Guandong province was the major manifestation of Kambrook's activities in Asia. In fact, this represented only one aspect of a complex of importing and exporting deals in the region. So, to provide infrastructural support for his company's activities, Bannigan opened a Hong Kong office in 1989.

New Zealand is the other major centre of Kambrook' operations outside Australia. Early developments there wer prompted by New Zealand import restrictions which involved licences to bring products into the country. 'W set up a factory there and we exported product from New Zealand and, in return for that, we were granted licence to bring product into New Zealand, so we had a two-way trade operating from day one,' Bannigan says. 'That's been very good in that [the] factory is world competitive in the types of products it makes.' Kambrook has, in fact, upgraded its facilities, which are in Auckland, by building a $A4.3 million factory warehouse.

Bannigan regards New Zealand as a good place for Australian manufacturers to cut their export teeth. 'It's similar to doing business with one of the states in Australia,' he says. 'You've got a population of about 3.5 million people, people who live in a similar style to ourselves. They eat the same types of foods, they cook in a similar sort of way, their life style, leisure style, is very similar to Australia. So it's really a logical market for the Australian to target early in the piece.'

Bannigan travels frequently to New Zealand, Asia and Europe to check on his manufacturing and licensing operations and to check out the electrical-goods market. He now generates sales of around $50 million a year outside Australia. But he is constantly on the lookout for new opportunities at home and overseas. In 1989, he announced Kambrook's entry into the computer market in Australia. He could see no reason to be overawed by the major international companies which have dominated information technology in Australia. On past performance, he will challenge them just as aggressively as he has the electrical giants.

Maggie Shepherd is another Australian who has made it in export from a humble start and without qualifications. And, with a mixture of political dryness and anarchic practicality, she is proud of it: 'We should start thinking differently in Australia. People should know that they don't really have to be an employee of somebody. You know, most kids when I went to school, we all thought, what kind of job can I get when I grow up, what kind of employee can I be? In fact, people don't have to be an employee; they can employ themselves.

'I did it with absolutely no training, no kind of specialised skills in this area, with the exception of all of the skills I've learned in the school of the world over a number of years, and with very little money, a miniscule amount of money. And I'd like to get across to kids who are in school: you don't have to have all of these qualifications that your parents keep telling you that you have to have and, your teachers believe, you will be a total failure, if you don't have. If you've got ability and a bit of drive and a bit of commonsense, then people can actually employ themselves. And don't we need that—people who can do things for themselves, instead of a pile of people who sit around and believe that the state really has to look after them? We've got to be responsible for ourselves, haven't we?'

As soon as she makes this point, she protects herself from pomposity by telling her interviewer: 'You don't want that load of rubbish. Rub that out.' Maggie Shepherd's sudden burst of amused self-deprecation lies lightly over the serious purpose of a shrewd and ambitious person. She is like a cyclist who hides the determination to win a big race behind the occasional tomfoolery of 'no-hands' riding.

This leads to some paradoxical positions. Take researching markets, for example. On the one hand, there is apparent nonchalance: 'There's only one kind of market research and that is if [people] pay their money for what you show them. You can go round and say, "What do you think of this?" and they can say, "Oh, very, very nice" not to upset you, but if they're not willing to put the cash down, then you're not to know, are you?' On the other hand, in discussing a hoped-for move into Japan, she will talk about the need to investigate the market in terms of what the Japanese want to buy and how to sell it to them. She is not about to rush in without a lot of careful planning.

What Maggie Shepherd sells in great quantity, both in Australia and in the United States, is clothes—colourful upmarket women's fashion garments. Her bold use of colour in some ways reflects the devil-may-care side of her. But the rapid spread and the location of her retail outlets reveal the determined and ambitious flipside. By the end of 1989 she had seven of her own stores in Australia and nine in the United States, in such places as Dallas, Baltimore, Chicago and Atlanta and just outside Washington and New York City. Each US store has been chosen because it is in a shopping centre with among the highest sales per square foot of retailing in the country. Together, the American shops generate annual sales of about $US4 million.

There will be many more Maggie Shepherd stores, if she has her way. 'We're concentrating on the US really,' she says. 'We're going to kind of cover the US as thickly as we possibly can so that's going to take a number of years. We're opening stores at about the rate of three a year and I suppose we'll open them a bit faster than that as time goes on.'

The remarkable thing is that she only started the business in 1980—in her Canberra home. She had been born in Canberra and, after leaving school, had worked in fashion retailing, designed window displays and spent a period in London where she designed and sold some original clothes. But, back in Australia, marriage took her away from fashion. But only for a while.

'I had two little children and a very large mortgage and I suddenly realised I had child endowment being put into my bank account every week,' she recalls. 'And I thought, what can I do with this $34 a week that can possibly change my situation in life? Having been able to sew—not very well but I was still able to sew—I went and bought some fabric, made up some clothes, went over to the local pre-school one day and asked everybody back for a cup of coffee and presented them with my very cheap and very poorly made range of clothes, which were kind of low in quality but high in imagination—and they all decided to buy. I started off a business at home and I had a lot of people coming to knock on the back door and buy things from me.'

In 1981, she and her husband, Bill, decided to open the first Shepherds store in Canberra. Within 18 months, they opened a Sydney shop. Stores in Brisbane, Adelaide, Surfers Paradise, Perth and Melbourne, plus a second shop in Sydney, followed. From the start, her clothes combined colour with an eclectic choice of fabrics, often featuring theatrical designs. Her shops also developed a distinctive, dramatic style: with black faux marble columns highlighting the colour of her fashions.

While her clothes are striking, she does not try to follow fashion trends. 'I suppose I've observed fashion over a number of years and fabrics come along and they suggest designs to me,' she says. 'I'm interested in the fashions of the times, even though the clothes I make aren't . . . *the* fashion at any given time. I just buy fabrics I like the look of and make them into things I like and I think other people will like and enjoy wearing.'

Her first two shops laid some of the groundwork for her eventual move into the United States. In Canberra, a friend and enthusiast for her clothes was an English resident, Susan Gilligan. She moved to the US in the 1980s and took not only some of the clothes with her but also a certain evangelism for them. Visiting Americans were among the customers of her Sydney store and this helped develop an interest in the possibilities of the US market.

The Shepherds took the plunge in 1986 when they decided to open a store at Tysons Corner, McLean, Virginia. Then came Atlanta, Baltimore, Dallas and one at Short Hills, New Jersey, not far from New York City. Bill Shepherd and Susan Gilligan chose the locations and Gilligan looked after promotion. It has suited Maggie Shepherd to leave on-the-ground supervision of the US operations to them, so that she can get on with her design work (and, as another factor avoid flying). While her husband travels to the US at leas twice a year, Maggie Shepherd, as noted earlier, did not go there until mid-1989.

Having her own stores has been an important part of her export strategy. It has meant that she has been able to keep her expansion into the US at a rate consistent with her company's financial and manufacturing ability. Control of her own retailing has eliminated the risks which would have been involved in wholesaling or franchising—risks such as being at the mercy of fickle store buyers. 'This can make forward planning of production a nightmare,' she says of this fickleness. 'Unlike those companies who wholesale internationally, we have outlets that require steady supplies of our product, and our company is therefore able to pursue a steadily increasing growth, and is always able to produce the goods when needed. This is something that many Australian companies have been unable to achieve when faced with huge orders that they have not experienced in their native Aussie market.'

Susan Gilligan said that Shepherds were very careful to identify their market before opening in the US. 'We spent a lot of time doing that before we came here because there is massive competition here in no matter what area,' she says. Maggie Shepherd might have established an identity in Australia but that had not carried through to the US.

'Nobody knows who Maggie Shepherd is in America, so you cannot use that as a selling point,' says Gilligan. 'You've got to go in another direction. The direction we went in was Australia. Everybody in America obviously has heard in the last two years—thanks to Paul Hogan—about Australia and it's a big selling point so, instead of pushing Maggie in the beginning, we pushed Australia . . . People would stop and say, "Is this really Australian? Don't they walk around in loin cloths and carry spears or something?" But they wanted to know, is this really Australian. That was our selling point.

'Now we've got people interested in the clothes, we are trying to identify Maggie as a person and because obviously in the end, if we're going to be successful—Australia is not always going to be the flavour of the month—we have to move on to the designer and that's what we're trying to do now.'

Maggie Shepherd points out that there is 'nothing particularly Australian about what I design'. 'I'm selling clothes which have got an international appeal,' she says, but then she qualifies that: 'There's one thing that makes our clothes vaguely different to clothes anywhere else in the world. It has got a slight Australian kind of look about it. [It] is the fact that they've got lots of vibrant colour in them and Europeans don't use colour in any great sense . . . Australians often use designs that are from Europe but we always bung a bit more colour in because the sunshine makes colour look so beautiful . . .

'People are attracted to attractive colours. They want to look nice and if everything was made in mud brown, I wouldn't sell many dresses, and the fact that our clothes are colourful and look attractive in the shop and the colour is very eye-catching draws people into the shop and makes them want to buy the dresses.'

The colour, in combination with bold designs, provides her explanation for her export success: 'You've got to have something that the rest of the world wants. We're selling things that really have no equivalent in America and being successful because of it.' That, combined with a keen-eyed selection of her market: 'We are selling to a small percentage of the market; we are specialising.'

Given the size of the US market, even a small percentage means considerable business. And there are other markets. Maggie Shepherd projects her nonchalant side as she contemplates the possibilities: 'I didn't plan I'm going to do this with my life, and I don't think anybody does. These things happen to you and, when I was doing it at home, I could have thought, well, this is a great way of earning a living; I'll make three dresses a week and that'll be a little bit of money which helps towards the housekeeping. But I thought if I can sell one or two, then I can sell three or four. It's only a matter of doubling it all the time as an economic decision to make the most of what I was able to do. And there's really no limit to what I can do and how far the business can go, and it would be very restrictive thinking to just stop in one spot.'

She explains her foreseeable ambitions: 'After America our main aim is Japan and that'll take much more time and it's a much greater effort, [with] more investigation of really what the Japanese want to buy—because, when you go to Japan, you notice that people tend to wear monotones black and white and grey, and we sell very bright clothes I don't think that matters really but we've got to know how to sell it to them and we'd like to have our own shops there also, which is a horrendously expensive exercise . . .

'In fact, we've had a fashion parade up there . . . and lot of respected ladies in Japanese society went along t it and it was reasonably successful. We had to make th clothes about one-third smaller because they're smaller people and we sold quite well. A lot of our fabrics are made of polyester which we find ideal for the Australian and American market, for price and also for usefulness, but we have a feeling that the Japanese want natural fibres, silk. If so, we might have to make a special range for them.'

It is her intention to continue manufacturing in Australia, despite overseas expansion, but she might modify that view. 'We could possibly manufacture in Asia,' she says. 'That's the only other place I think we could manufacture [our clothes]. We've found it okay to manufacture in Australia and it's very good being able to manufacture where you are and you really control the whole process. If things are a long way away, then you're a little bit out of control. You don't know whether the legs are being sewed together or whether the arms are being put in the leg hole or whatever until it actually arrives in the shop and they say, "Look, this is a mistake", and you've got 10 000 of them. So it is useful to manufacture them where you are but, of course, economics will dictate, at some stage, we might manufacture off shore.'

Maggie Shepherd contemplates her life now with satisfaction: 'I do love the business side of it. I don't really have any trouble doing the designing side and it takes infinitely less, [it's a] smaller part of my life than people would imagine. They think that I kind of sit there and labour over designs endlessly and I know other designers seem to. It's kind of one-tenth of the amount of time I spend on the business. I just like the interest of business and the interest of making it grow as big and as complex as it possibly can because . . . it's exciting. There are times when things aren't going so well—you're not so interested in it. Then you think, let's sell up and go away. But the exciting times, when you're received well and it's a success—great.'

With four expensive imported cars in the family garage of a stylish home, she responds to a question about her attitude to money: 'I think the passion to make money is great. That's the business side of me, I suppose, but also making money doing something that's creative—that's very nice; it's very good for the soul.'

Frank Seeley started out with the attitudes to export of the average Australian manufacturer—not those of Heimo Eberhardt, Frank Bannigan or Maggie Shepherd. He had achieved a prominent position in the Australian market as a maker of portable evaporative air-conditioners. His factory was busy with the growing domestic demand for his products. Why bother to try to venture into the unknown?

His Assistant General Manager, Murray Morton, thought differently. It was not because of any special background: Morton was a former electrician who had joined Seeley when he began manufacturing operations in Adelaide in 1972. He had never exported anything in his life. But he believed that, in the long term, Seeley would need export markets to ensure continued growth. He proposed to Seeley that they investigate foreign markets. Seeley rejected the idea: they had enough on their plate at home without being bothered by overseas expansion.

Then Morton learned that the Australian Government made export marketing development grants which would cover a large part of the cost of an overseas trip. He put it to Seeley that the company could therefore well afford to send him on an exploratory journey. Reluctantly, Seeley agreed: Morton could go overseas for one month.

That was to be the turning point for the company. Now appropriately called Seeley International, it has become the world's largest manufacturer of portable evaporative air conditioners. And it has recently made significant inroads into the market for rooftop evaporative air-conditioners. It has also transformed Murray Morton's life. Frank Seeley is the kind of person who believes that, if someone picks up a ball and runs with it, you don't take it away while it's still in play. So Murray Morton is now Seeley International's export manager and spends as much as five or six months a year travelling overseas.

Into the story of the company's move into export should not be read the meaning that Frank Seeley is a timid man. He is not. From the start of his business life, the indications have been otherwise.

A jovial, bearded bear of a man, his first occupation was schoolteaching but, in his twenties, he went into business with his brother to sell evaporative air-conditioners on commission. His brother died young. Still only in his late twenties, Frank Seeley shouldered the responsibility of having with two families, including ten children, to support. He needed a substantial income to meet their needs so he threw himself into commission selling with as much vigour as he could muster. By the early 1970s, he was turning over about $1 million worth of air-conditioners each year.

The company which was producing the air-conditioners decided he was making too much money so it told him it would halve his commission. Infuriated, Seeley announced that he would manufacture his own air-conditioners. He borrowed $20 000 for six months in 1972 and set about coming up with a rival product.

Although he had no formal technical training, Seeley brought to the task ideas that were going to change manufacturing in his field. The product he had been selling on commission had 386 parts, including 187 metal parts. Because evaporative air-conditioners are kept cool with water, rusting of the metal parts was a fundamental maintenance problem. He also thought that the large number of parts unnecessarily complicated the manufacturing task and added to costs. So he set about reducing the number of parts and replacing as many of the metal parts as possible with plastic to minimise the corrosion problem.

He took his ideas to a toolmaker and, despite the scepticism of many in the industry, achieved his objectives. He came up with an air-conditioner with 56 parts, including only seven metal parts. His reliance on plastic was the most controversial part of his products. His rivals labelled Seeley a 'backyarder' and said plastic did not have the necessary durability. In fact, because of its anticorrosive properties, it proved itself more durable than metal. (Later, when Seeley used plastic as the main component of rooftop air-conditioners, his rivals said it would distort, even melt, due to its exposure to changing weather. Seeley beat that charge by giving a ten-year structural warranty on the units.)

He moved into a little factory in the Adelaide suburb of Edwardstown and began manufacturing the first of a long line of Convair and Breezair air-conditioners. Because of the savings in parts, he had an immediate cost advantage. But, he points out, the product was superior in other ways: 'We came up with a product which delivered more air, which had a higher saturation or cooling efficiency, which drew half the power and made half the noise of the previous unit.' In his first year of manufacture, he sold 1000 units.

By 1976, he was selling 7000 air-conditioners. Then, in September 1976, his factory burned down right at the start of his selling season. He promised his 30 workers that he would be back in production in a week. When this was reported on a local television news broadcast, he was inundated with offers of help. His promise was kept. Five weeks later, five separate fires were found burning in his new premises at St Marys, Adelaide. It was clearly arson and Seeley had a pretty good idea who was behind it although no one was ever arrested. Again, the factory was back in production in a week.

Then, in 1979, Murray Morton left on his first oversea trip to try to sell Seeley products. He started in the United States and, in the beginning, was somewhat overawed by the difficulty of breaking into such a market. After a week Seeley considered bringing him home. That possibility gave Morton an extra incentive and his confidence quickl returned. He followed a tip and went to Iraq, a countr with the kind of dry heat in which evaporative air-coole are most appropriate. A government purchasing agenc showed apparent interest, so he left a sample behind.

Three months later, a call from Iraq summoned Morto and Seeley back to the Middle East. They were treated some not-so-delicate negotiating games, such as being ke waiting three and a half hours for a key meeting. But th emerged with an order for 20 000 portable air-conditioner

Given that Seeley was then producing about 18 000 uni a year for the Australian market, it meant that he had more than double production immediately. If that p pressure on his production line, it was nothing compar to his dilemma when, in 1981, the Iraqis ordered a furth 100 000 air-conditioners: 'When we obtained that order, got our people together and we said, "It's not going to easy. We're going to have to do two assembly shifts" .

We got our suppliers together and we said, "Right, you're going to have to perform better than you ever have before." And everyone came to the party and the net result was that we were able to produce 1500 coolers per day off our two assembly lines.'

From the earliest days, Seeley has kept improving the design and refining the manufacture of his air-conditioners. Importantly, he has protected himself by registering each technical advance and he has had quite a number. And there has been the constant search for cost-savings—to the point that the manufacturing cost of each portable cooler is now lower than it was in 1972.

In 1979, one big saving was forced upon him. The supplier of the specialised motors for his air-conditioners had a monopoly and was confronting Seeley with unacceptable price rises. So Seeley decided to make his own. It cost him $1 million to install plant to do the job but he saved $10 on each motor. Within 12 months, he received the Iraqi order for 100 000 units and thus recouped his capital cost almost immediately.

Seeley regards this kind of vertical integration as a key to his success: 'It has allowed us to maintain unmatchable quality control—an extremely important factor when you're establishing markets far from home.'

The second Iraqi order lifted Seeley's revenues to $16.2 million in 1981-82. To help cope with the increased demand and in anticipation of future orders, Seeley decided to build a factory in Singapore to make 20 000 to 30 000 units a year. It was not quite completed when the Iran-Iraq war broke out. Suddenly, his best customer was no more. Revenues went into reverse and Seeley had no choice but to drop his Singapore manufacturing plans; he leased the factory there to a Japanese company.

At the same time, this setback forced him to look urgently for new markets. And he found them—in Europe, the United States and Asia. He now exports to about 30 countries. In the US, he has established a sub-assembly plant in Denison, on the banks of the Red River in Texas. There, electrical components are put into the rooftop units, which are otherwise made in Adelaide. Portable air-conditioners are still wholly made in Adelaide but are distributed from Denison. In the UK, Seeley has established a marketing office to service Europe. He is planning to establish a modest manufacturing facility in Europe so he is not shut out by any trade barriers after EEC unification in 1992.

Seeley International has not neglected the Australian market. It claims 80 per cent of the local market in portable evaporative air-conditioners and 65 per cent of the rooftop market here. But it does even more of its business in foreign markets. The balance in 1989 was about 60 per cent of sales overseas and 40 per cent in Australia.

Frank Seeley and Murray Morton have not disagreed about export in ages.

Heimo Eberhardt, Frank Bannigan, Maggie Shepherd and Frank Seeley have a number of vital things in common as exporters.

First, although Frank Seeley might have needed a push-start, all of them have a strong commitment to exporting as a key, even predominant, element of their businesses. Second, they all bring great drive and enthusiasm to developing foreign markets. An aspect of this is that they either travel a lot themselves, or have partners or senior executives who do.

All have expanded overseas after establishing a solid domestic base, although, in Eberhardt's case, the home market has become a very minor part of his trading activities.

It is noticeable that they have carefully identified their market segments and concentrated their energy on those areas. Since he started out, Frank Seeley might have added rooftop air-conditioners to portable air-coolers but all his products rely on basically the same technology. Maggie Shepherd focuses on a narrow, upmarket segment of the fashion market. Frank Bannigan has a number of products to which he keeps adding, but all are household appliances which combine innovation with utility. Heimo Eberhardt still bases much of his business on spectrometry and related fields. Computers were initially a spin-off from spectrometry. Now that Labtam has established a reputation in computers he is developing new markets for his information technology

All of them have been prepared to pursue different means of getting their products into their target markets. None of them relies totally on simply making a product and then sending off quantities of it to an agent or distributor. Frank Bannigan has factories in Australia and New Zealand and exports from those countries; he licenses the manufacture of his appliances and components in the UK and China. Heimo Eberhardt exports directly from Australia and has initiated joint venture projects in the USSR and India. Frank Seeley mainly manufactures and exports from Australia but has a sub-assembly plant in the United States and is planning a small manufacturing operation in Europe. Maggie Shepherd avoids middlemen entirely by having her own retail outlets in the United States.

Finally, all of them devote a lot of time and money to improving their existing products or developing new ones. That is only to be expected from Maggie Shepherd as the women's fashion industry, of its very nature, demands constant innovation. But it is just as true of the others: research and development is a significant factor in their activities.

5 The Changing Workplace

MANY of Australia's problems as an exporter of manufactured products can be traced back to our factories, mills and workshops. Inefficiencies in the workplace have reduced quality, reliability and innovation and have increased costs. Australia is now struggling to overcome those deficiencies.

Sheltered for so long behind high protectionist walls, it is not surprising that our manufacturing industry became inefficient. Managers looked out on assured markets and so had little incentive to keep costs low and quality high provided they kept both within vaguely acceptable bounds they still sold their products. The protected environment also encouraged perks and pay concessions to their workforce, particularly as an overriding objective was industrial peace—often at the expense of industrial efficiency. Finally, in a non-competitive environment managers were under little pressure to update their plant. Complacency bred obsolescence.

For its part, the workforce was formed into a multitude of narrow union groupings which, derived from England, had changed little for decades. Demands for higher wages and better conditions did not need to be justified by increased productivity. Rather they reflected long-established battles between unions and management on how to carve up the financial cake.

At the same time, the traditional union groupings bred demarcation disputes: members of one union would seek the exclusive right to perform certain types of work. Not only did inter-union rivalry cause industrial stoppages but also some very strange divisions of labour. An operator from one union might have to sit around waiting for a maintenance worker from another to repair a machine which any ordinarily useful person could fix with a turn of a wrench. Or a skilled metal tradesman might be kept idle until an electrician came to change a blown light bulb.

Even within unions, there were divisions of members into innumerable work classifications, involving demarcation barriers which affected the way in which people could work. As late as 1989, one Sydney factory was notorious for having 300 award classifications to cover only 1000 employees. They represented an accumulation of narrow advantages, sometimes to the benefit of the employees, sometimes to the company.

The old demarcation rigidities have limited the skills of our workforce. Production workers have been locked into dead-end jobs with little or no incentive to add to their skills. And, too often, tradespeople have not progressed beyond their initial qualifications. A generation ago, those qualifications might have served them through to retirement but, even then, many would not have worked to the full potential of their talents. And now those initial qualifications will not be enough for a full working life because of changing technology.

In December 1987, the Australian Science and Technology Council (ASTEC) declared in a report to the Prime Minister, *Education and National Needs*: 'Australia is underskilled'. It added: 'Given the low level of training by industry itself, the skills of Australia's secondary industry workforce are lower than those of other countries with comparable wages.'

It has all added up to a sorry picture: inefficient, outdated factories, with complacent owners and managers and with inflexible workforces given limited opportunities for advancement. If Australian manufacturing industry was to become internationally competitive, it had to change. Fortunately, it is changing. But whether the process happens quickly enough and goes far enough will be one of the great microeconomic challenges facing Australia in the next few years.

The pattern of change has been varied and fragmented.

Some unions—such as the Amalgamated Metal Workers Union (AMWU), the Federated Ironworkers Association (FIA) and the Vehicle Builders Employees Federation (VBEF)—have been active; others resistant. It has been the same with employers.

While those involved have come from across the political spectrum, the movement for change has made for some strange bedfellows. In some manufacturing areas, left-wing unions have swung from the status of pariahs to being seen almost as the helpmates of industry. This has occurred where rival unions have built complex structures of sweetheart deals involving 'soft' work practices and have been reluctant to let anyone tamper with them. Sections of the left have been the most willing participants in trade-offs for improved work practices and higher productivity on the one hand and, on the other, benefits—ranging from higher pay to better career opportunities—for their members.

The supreme symbol of this curious swing is Laurie Carmichael, who used to run the AMWU before he became Assistant Secretary of the ACTU, where he has a special responsibility for workplace reform. His transition from radical ogre to apostle of efficiency has been described in chapter 1. Some business leaders refer to him as 'the new Laurie Carmichael'. He resists the implication that he has somehow abandoned his earlier views: 'I've changed certainly, but it's been more of an evolution than . . . sudden switch.' And when he surveys Australian management's role in increasing investment, in training and the encouragement of quality, he cannot resist taking a swipe at his old foes:

'I don't think management has led too much in this country and I think the workforce has led management lot more than what would have normally been expected. However, our living standards are at stake and, if we [the workforce] don't do it, then it's our living standards that will suffer. So we can't hang around waiting for management to catch up with the rest of the world. We've got to force the issue and the workforce needs to use its organised strength, its political clout, its capability in the workplace in order to press the issue forward, if we want continual expanding living standards . . . The only way we can do it is to force the issue, compel management, compel industry to upgrade its act despite itself.'

Not everyone would accept all of Carmichael's ideas but there is agreement—in government and unions and among employers—that change is needed. It is clear that there is no single reform which will fix Australia's workplace problems, no room for simple-minded solutions such as banning strikes.

Broadly, most parties to this debate in Australia would agree that Australia needs a more efficient workforce—where unnecessary barriers are broken down between types of jobs, new ways of working are explored, management is improved, better communication is opened up and new career paths offer performance and training incentives. Linked to this, we also need a more skilled—and more *flexibly* skilled— workforce so that industry can respond to new challenges and opportunities. Finally, we need to improve the work environment, so that ageing plant is replaced and new manufacturing techniques are introduced.

The rest of this chapter looks at companies within several industries where at least some of these needs are being met. All of the companies had little choice: workplace change was a precondition of survival. Some of them have found new profitability; others still have some battles in front of them. But it has helped all of them aim for either export or import-replacement—or both.

Few sectors of Australian manufacturing have caused more heartaches for both consumers and governments than the automotive industry. Prices have been too high and quality too low. Australian-made cars were an endangered species, preserved behind high tariff walls.

The Australian Government stepped in in 1984 with the Passenger Motor Vehicle Manufacturing Plan, commonly called the 'Button Plan' after the Minister, Senator John Button, who initiated it. Among its objectives: a drop in the number of manufacturer groups from 5 to 3; a reduction in the number of models produced here from 13 to 6 or less; efficiencies achieved through improved capacity utilisation and increased model volumes; better productivity and more competitiveness; improved quality. It is a package intended to give Australian consumers a better deal and to boost exports of both cars and components.

It has had a limited degree of success. The Automotive Industry Authority (AIA), set up to administer the plan, reported in 1989 on the rationalisation of producer groupings along the right lines. A joint venture agreement between AMI Toyota and Holden's involved model and facility sharing; Ford and Nissan were pursuing a model sharing agreement, with Ford also having a major export program; and Mitsubishi, standing alone, was relying on exports to increase output volumes. The *Sydney Morning Herald* of 11 June 1988 reported on one practical effect of this: 'All Holdens by the mid 1990s will be rebadged Toyotas sold through the joint venture company set up by Toyota and General Motors. The company credited with starting it all in the 1950s, GM-H, will sink slowly into the sunset.'

By the end of 1989, the number of models produced in Australia had dropped to eight. But Australia was still well short of an appropriate overseas model of efficiency, Sweden where two carmakers, Volvo and Saab, very profitably make only four models. And, according to the AIA report, there was still a long way to go before other key aspects of the Button Plan were fulfilled.

Investment expenditure has been substantial: with more than $2 billion spent from 1985 to 1988 and a further $2. billion expected from 1989 to 1992. But the AIA notes that indications are that not enough of this money has been spent on automation and more advanced manufacturing technologies. Automation in Australian car factories is well under half that achieved in Japan, the United States or Europe.

Motor vehicle prices have risen by more than the rate of inflation since the inception of the Button Plan. Productivity continues to lag: it is half that of Japanese and American factories. Labour turnover is even more out of kilter with the rest of the world: Australia has an average annual turnover of 35 per cent of automotive employees; the national group with the second worst rate is US-owned plants in North America where the average turnover rate is only 7 per cent.

Finally, quality remains a major problem. The AIA published figures showing the average number of faults reported for locally produced and imported vehicle models from mid-1984 to mid-1988. In all categories—small, medium and large—Australian models were far behind the imports. The average number of faults in local cars came into the following range: small cars, 1.93 to 2.86; medium, 2.21 to 2.82; and large, 2.86 to 3.37. The figures for comparable fully imported models were: small cars, 1.18; medium, 1.36; and large, 1.41.

The AIA made this comment: 'Before the [Button] Plan ends in 1992, it is essential that the current gap between the quality of locally manufactured cars and those produced by our international competitors is substantially narrowed if the Australian PMV [Passenger Motor Vehicle] industry is to be viable under lower levels of assistance.' It adds, with a hint of chin-up optimism: 'There is no doubt that the narrowing of the quality gap remains one of the greatest challenges facing the local industry as it moves towards 1992. The quality achievements of Japanese firms building cars in the United States market show that this challenge can be met.'

Still, there are glimmers of hope. Adelaide-based Mitsubishi Australia has ventured into a 'coals-to-Newcastle' exercise by exporting Magna station wagons to Japan. At this stage, it is a very small operation: only about 30 or so Magnas are sold there each month.

But Bill Scales, AIA Chairman and Chief Executive, nominates it as a clever example of niche marketing. Because of the narrowness of their streets, Japanese drivers have never gone in for large American cars. With growing affluence, however, more Japanese are getting into outdoor leisure activities, such as skiing and family outings. As a result, some of them want a bigger than normal vehicle and that's the market the Magna is aimed at. While it is not a large car by American standards, it is advertised as the 'Big Wagon from Mitsubishi Motors Australia'. Far from there being attempt to pass it off as a Japanese-made vehicle, a kangaroo decal is emblazoned on the side of the vehicle. And, interestingly, it is selling into the upper end of the market as a high-priced product.

It is this kind of marketing expertise that has helped Mitsubishi to profitability. In fact, Mitsubishi was one of only two Australian companies—the other is Ford—to make a profit out of car manufacturing operations in 1988.

The Magna sales are only the tip of an iceberg for Mitsubishi Australia in Japan. Its biggest export business is a deal, worth $14 million a year, to supply its parent company in Japan with blocks, engines, cylinder heads and other automotive components.

It has taken much more than good marketing to put Mitsubishi Australia into profit. Workplace reform has also been a major element in its success. Organisation of its 4000 workers into teams, greater emphasis on quality control on the shopfloor, improved communication and the promotion of skills have been its central features. The company's factories in the Adelaide suburbs of Tonsley Park and Lonsdale have come a long way since Mitsubishi took them over from the ailing Chrysler Corporation a decade ago.

A new era started with Mitsubishi's introduction of a no-retrenchment policy in 1980. Even in lean times, the company is committed to keeping on its workers. The policy was introduced after two successive years of lay-offs. Assembly plant manager, John Vine, had to organise the sackings: 'I did that two years in a row just before I went on holiday and I did not enjoy my holiday. Since that time, we've said to people, "We will no longer have retrenchment programs. If the volume should change, we will wear the problem. You have got a job as long as you want to work here. As long as you're prepared to produce the quality that we want you've got a job." And that was a fundamental change [in the way this company thought about people, so we then realised that we must look after people if we expect them to look after us . . . If you want people to be loyal to you you've got to be loyal to them and it's no use buying and selling people just as you would a herd of cattle.'

Harry Davies, Welsh immigrant, former shop steward and now in charge of a rehabilitation unit for injured and sick workers, has worked with Chrysler and then Mitsubishi for about 20 years. He believes that the no-retrenchment policy led to a fundamental change in attitude on both sides: 'I honestly believe that worker and management have realised that you've got to survive and to survive you've got to work together. And the bottom line, as I see it, is that if you don't, we'll be back into the days when Chryslers were here and there won't be any jobs.'

Mitsubishi's next step was to set about getting rid of old production-line work methods. No longer does each worker perform one narrow procedure by himself. Instead, the workforce is organised into groups, each responsible for a major section of the vehicles they are producing. Every member of every group is encouraged to think in terms of quality. John Vine summarises this approach: 'We've got to be quite scrupulous in every phase of our activities, from the smallest part through to the coat of paint, to every screw we attach to the car. Everything must be done correctly. Everyone that plays a part in that process has got to do their bit . . . Once whatever you could get past the inspector was good enough. For today, that's no longer good enough.

'Without quality, we cannot compete in the world marketplace. We believe we've a product as good as anything in Australia but that's not where we need to sell. We need to sell in the world.'

Within each group of 10–15 people is a quality checker. He not only inspects the work of his own group, he is a member of a 'quality circle'. This is a Japanese concept which brings key workers from different areas together to compare notes on matters affecting quality. Members of quality circles are generally experienced assembly-line workers who know what goes into building a car and where problems are most likely to occur. Their knowledge and experience has been turned into a resource to help the company improve quality and cut costs.

The quality circles also make regular presentations of their ideas to audiences combining management and workers. These can be somewhat awkward affairs as the presenters are people trained in mechanical skills, not public relations. But that does not matter if they get results. And they can.

A presentation might involve explaining the importance of correctly fitting a single bolt into a bracket on the chassis. But its importance becomes obvious when the presenter explains that every incorrectly fitted bolt costs $75 in labour and materials to replace and demonstrates how that can add up to $40 000 a year. A presentation like that every week would be welcome in any company.

These presentations are indicative of a new approach by Mitsubishi towards management–worker communication. Harry Davies has noticed the difference: 'I think really that management are prepared to come and talk to people now, where in the past they weren't. They come and talk to people on the jobs and I think that the worker on the shopfloor, before he does anything drastic, reallises that he can talk to people first and try to get something resolved. Before, there was a great division between management and working on the shopfloor.'

'I could go back to 10 years ago when we didn't have that goodwill,' John Vine says. 'It was a case of trying to drive them to do a job and it's part of our basic philosophy that we try and lead people now to achieve the task and get them encouraged in the job they're doing so that they feel part of the team . . . We have really been heartened to see the way in which people can grow. They get not only the immediate satisfaction of seeing the product improve but they get an opportunity to work in teams, develop leadership skills and allow themselves to grow so that, while we can build a better product, we can also build a bette. person.'

A much more sudden example of workplace change in the automotive industry has been brought about by another Japanese-owned company, Toyota. It has involved taking over where GM-H, the old flagship of the Australian industry, left off.

GM-H had a long-established plant in the Melbourn suburb of Dandenong. After watching its losses grow, the company decided in 1987 to bite the bullet: it gave a year' notice that, come the end of 1988, the factory would close Its 900 employees would lose their jobs. The GM-H withdrawal went ahead and the last Holden Camira came off the Dandenong assembly line in December 1988. But, by then, the fortunes of the factory and its workforce were about to change for the better. Toyota was taking both over.

Not everyone was sure how they felt about that at first. Former senior shop steward Vern Shukowski recalls that he was going to pay off his mortgage with his redundancy compensation. That was not to be: 'There was a bit of an uproar then because people had got used to the idea of having their redundancy money and now, all of a sudden, they had a job again.' Not only did the old GM-H employees have a job but so eventually did another 300 people: by mid-1989 the workforce had grown to 1200.

Toyota moved into Dandenong in January 1989 and immediately began a $30 million refurbishment of the old factory. When it re-opened, it even ran to carpet on the shopfloor. As a first basis for a new efficiency of operation, Toyota gave its employees a modern environment in which to work.

The factory is being used to produce Corollas for Toyota and, comforming to the rationalisation sought by the Button Plan, Novas for GM-H; essentially the same car with different badges. The first car, a new style Corolla, came off the assembly line in April 1989 and the model was launched publicly in June.

More important than the launching of a new model—and a vital accompaniment to the factory rebuilding—was Toyota's introduction of a new way of working. The Toyota Production System is the combination of methods by which has produced cars so successfully in Japan. As with Mitsubishi, it is based on organising the workforce into teams.

At Toyota the teams are small—eight to ten people. The new system involves a big change from the American-style production methods with which employees at Dandenong were familiar. It involves an entirely different approach to hierarchy, with each member of a production team responsible for his or her own safety, time-keeping, inventory-control, maintenance and the like. Any member of a team can stop the production line if concerned about quality. This means that everyone, including the least skilled personnel, has greater decision-making powers, responsibility and involvement.

To prepare the workforce and while the factory refurbishment proceeded, Toyota sent 65 of its employees to Japan to see the production system in operation in Toyota plants there. They were drawn from varying levels, including foremen, supervisors and tradespeople. Vern Shukowski, now a group leader with about 30 people divided into three teams working under him, was one of those who went to Japan. The trip, he says, 'showed us that they [Toyota] were really committed to making the project work at Dandenong.'

The trip immediately brought home the difference in attitudes to work between Japan and Australia. 'In Japan, it was a real eye-opener to see how they operated over there, compared to what I was used to under Holdens. The Japanese have a different work ethic or culture . . . Someone asks you where you work in Japan and you tell them you work at Toyota, they say, "Oh, terrific, you must be proud to work for a company like that", whereas in Australia, if someone asked you where you worked and you told them you worked at Toyota, they'd think, oh, that's a bit of a bummer of a job . . .

'The workers there are a lot more committed to working for Toyota and getting the cars out. There, they get to work a lot earlier. The line might start at 8 o'clock. They will start at quarter to eight, filling up the line, making sure their guns are working, and, once that whistle goes at 8 o'clock, they work. They have a 10-minute tea-break. A lot of them keep working through the tea-break and until they have their area spot on, then they'll go for their cup of tea. They don't automatically stop where, in Australia, as soon as the whistle goes, everyone's off for tea-break, tools down and off they go . . .

'There's a lot of things that I wouldn't want to see in Australia because it's a different culture but I think a lot of things we can learn from and, if we don't, then we won't be able to compete and there'll be factories closed in this country.'

Shukowski was impressed by Japanese productivity: 'They built one car in every 57 seconds. I think at Holden's we

were down to about a minute and 30 seconds but, to get
it down to 57 seconds will take a big effort from everyone.
Whether we will get it to that level remains to be seen.'

As for quality, he believes Toyota is headed in the right
direction in Australia: 'I think the [component makers] who
supply us with material have a long way to go. Once they
get their act together, combined with the efforts of the vehicle
manufacturers, I think we can compete quality-wise.'

It is too early to say how well the Toyota production
system will work in Australia. But Vern Shukowski is
convinced it is the way to go: 'You can always learn from
someone else and the Japanese learned that a long time ago.
They weren't embarrassed about copying things but they
didn't just copy them. They always improved them and one
of the things that the Japanese, especially Toyota, have, is
a word which means "continual improvement". It doesn't
matter what you do, you've always got to improve on what
you've just improved. You can always do something better
and I think that once that gets instilled into the management,
the workers and the union movement—it'll take months,
maybe years . . . I think that's when we will win.'

While Australian car makers have found it difficult to adjust
to life with reduced protection, our shipbuilders have coped
better in less sheltered waters. They have abandoned trying
to compete against the rest of the world in producing big
ships. Instead, they have recognised that their best chance
of survival—even prosperity—is to concentrate on smaller
vessels, generally below 5000 tonnes.

It is starting to pay dividends. 'Australian shipbuilders
are establishing competitive niches in world markets in high-
speed ferries, luxury motor yachts and specialised fishing
vessels,' according to the 1987–88 annual report of the
Department of Industry, Technology and Commerce
(DITAC). 'The three-year plan to assist shipbuilding in
Australia, introduced in 1986, continued to bear fruit in
1987–88. The value of ships exported in 1985 was less than
$5 million; whereas, at 31 March 1988, vessels destined for
export accounted for $155 million out of a total production
$353 million.'

Workplace reform has played its part in the success. First of all, shipbuilding companies have introduced innovative techniques. 'Construction in other than traditional steel is a feature and Australian technology in some instances leads the world,' the DITAC report says. 'Investment in facilities and equipment continues to grow and there is a high use (more than 80 per cent) of Australian resources, a turnaround from last decade.' There have also been important changes in the way in which the workforce is employed.

'In some shipbuilding companies in Australia, the workplace reforms have been very significant and very successful,' Senator John Button, Minister for Industry, Technology and Commerce in the Hawke Government, says. 'But it depends on a good relationship between management and workforce so they mutually understand the importance of these problems. In some places, you have the trade union movement saying we want more training, we want better flexibility in the workforce, and management not being receptive to that. In other places, you have management saying that and the union movement not being receptive to it . . . I'm very encouraged by what is happening, but I think we've got a fair way to go.'

A good example of the industry's developing fortunes is North Queensland Engineers and Agents (NQEA). The company has not always built boats. In fact, it used to make machinery for sugar mills—that is, until the sugar industry hit a slump. To stay alive and avoid retrenchements, the company bid for a military contract for 11 landing craft for the Australian Army. It won the contract on the basis of its engineering skills.

'We have never, from that time onwards, considered shipbuilding to be a very complicated task and it's been part of us ever since,' says NQEA owner, Don Fry. 'We went into shipbuilding believing they were a queer-shaped box powered, and it did not require traditional skills or painters and dockers, shipwrights and many other skills and trades that were being used at that time. And so we went into it with about four basic trades—metal trades, electrician painters and crane drivers—and they are the skills that we still use today to build a boat.'

Fry's account makes it all sound so easy. In fact, the company has had to learn a lot to reach its present level of success. First, it had to develop skills in the use of aluminium, with which it has replaced steel as its shipbuilding material. It has done it and, in the process, become a world leader in aluminium technology in its field. (The aluminium, by the way, is made from bauxite mined not far away from Cairns, at Weipa, but is refined in the south and then sent back north for fabrication.)

The company also had much to learn about industrial relations. When it ran out of military work in the early 1980s, it hit lean times and, in 1984, tried to lay off 40 per cent of its workforce. A bitter union–management fight ensued and culminated in a 12-week strike. In a sense, the strike was the bloodletting that both sides needed: it forced them to sit down and sort out their differences.

The resulting agreements are pointed to—even by sections of the trade-union movement—as a model for industrial harmony and efficiency. There has been no industrial trouble since the 1984 strike. And award structures were negotiated to break down old work demarcations and to give NQEA's 600 employees new, multiple skills.

There is growing agreement—in government, unions and employer groups—that award restructuring is a vital element in the industrial reforms needed to make Australia more export-competitive. In 1989, the ACTU won union endorsement of the restructuring of a number of awards. Laurie Carmichael said of its efforts: 'What we're seeking to do by way of award restructuring would in many ways represent world leadership.' At the same time, the Hawke Government was giving the process considerable support. Prime Minister Hawke wrote to 3500 companies to seek their commitment to award restructuring.

Why is it seen to be so vital? First, it is aimed at cleaning up the messy patchwork of awards and agreements, often riddled with restrictive demarcations, bad work practices and sweetheart deals, which cover so many Australian workers. Take the metal trades award as an example. In a pamphlet written in terms likely to appeal most to its members, the AMWU put the case for restructuring the award. It said in part: 'There are over 300 classifications in the present award, most of which are based on the technology in use prior to the 1950s. While it retains classifications related to the steam engine era, it does not provide for metal workers who use computerised equipment or assemble micro-electronics. The old award was a product of the management ideas of the 1920s which emphasised controlling workers by dividing them into narrow skill classifications.' It could have added that workers often supported these classifications to maintain exclusivity of employment or other perks.

The pamphlet continued: 'The new award will provide for a career path from a base grade labourer or Metal Industry Worker I through nine classifications to an engineer. It will cover all aspects of work in the metal and engineering industry.' Combined with measures for ongoing training, metal trades workers will have the opportunity to progress more easily through the ranks. In addition, they will be able to work with a flexibility which should increase their productivity. Another AMWU circular gives the following examples: 'A machine operator should, after the correct training, be able to use a pendant crane to remove and install work into their machine. Alternatively, an electrician involved in a job which requires a small amount of welding work should be able to carry out this task, providing they have the required training.' So the electrician does some welding; and the welder does not have to sit around and wait for the electrician to replace a blown light bulb.

Peter Morris, Industrial Relations Minister in the Hawke Government, gave this summary of the benefits of award restructuring to the workforce in an interview: 'It makes them more efficient, more productive, it makes them more competitive and, most importantly, then we have people performing jobs that are more satisfying, more interesting, better paid and they've got a way to get ahead.'

It is this approach which has already made significant progress at NQEA. The company still runs an engineering shop for sugar mill machinery, as well as having a shipyard. A tradesperson working in the shipyard one day might be in the engineering shop the next. No one is tied to a single machine or task.

This is how one NQEA boilermaker explained it: 'Fifty years ago, the blokes wouldn't have read about the things we do now. They wouldn't believe it . . . Like boilermakers, you know—you wouldn't see a boilermaker go anywhere near a lathe or doing things that fitters would do, and fitters wouldn't be doing what boilermakers are doing. Now, you can get a fitter that will walk on to the job as a welder and train him up to be an aluminium welder straight up and all he's got to have is a fitter's ticket . . . Or he could even become a boilermaker; depends what they hire him for.' But, he said, not everyone liked the change.

It is, in fact, a feature of award restructuring in some factories that management and union officials might agree on it, only to find resistance in the workforce. The promise of training and better career paths can seem a bit elusive to some workers who are afraid that restructuring will take away their exclusive right to perform certain types of work.

Laurie Carmichael acknowledges that not all people in the union movement—including some officials—share his enthusiasm for award reform: 'Any new idea by definition starts with a minority of people, and the theory of strategy teaches you that you convert a minority into a majority and that requires time, it requires effort, it requires intellectual application. Now, we've been putting into place a number of catalytic things which are causing the debate to take place and gradually the union movement is coming around.'

At NQEA the best argument for restructuring has been the company's growing success. In 1989 it was undertaking a $10 million upgrading of its facilities. Since the days of military contracts, it has turned to catamaran ferries and motor yachts and is exporting them to the US, Europe, Papua New Guinea, New Zealand, Kuwait, Japan and Taiwan.

In June 1989, for example, it launched a catamaran ferry to run between Venice and Yugoslavia. NQEA delivered the ferry in only 18 weeks from the date of order. It cost $5 million, only one-third of the price of the Italian-built hydrofoil it has replaced. And its operating costs are half that of the hydrofoil. As this vessel was being launched, an $11 million motor yacht was being built for a Florida property developer. And only two months earlier, the New

South Wales Government had announced that it had placed with NQEA an order for three catamaran ferries, each costing $5.2 million and capable of carrying 250 passengers, to replace Sydney's trouble-prone hydrofoils on the Manly run in 1990.

Garry Steene, NQEA's executive director of marketing, is particularly enthusiastic about the sales potential of the ferries: 'Prospects for boats like this in Europe are absolutely astronomical. I've travelled right through Yugoslavia, Britain, Spain, Italy and Greece. There are virtually hundreds of very outdated, mainly hydrofoil-type, ferry boats and I think our wave-piercing catamaran is going to take that market by storm.'

To Don Fry, 'to export is to survive'. He believes his workforce is solidly behind that credo. 'Many people that started work here long ago thought that they would be building fairly agricultural type things and I can sense that many of the people here now get as much pride and pleasure out of seeing the ships that we build sail away as I do.'

Steelworks are the nearest thing we have to the dark, satanic mills of union demonology. Hot, dirty, noisy places, they can never be paradise for workers. But in the Newcastle foundries of Comsteel, a subsidiary of the Australian National Industries (ANI) group, major changes are happening. And they've turned an unprofitable operation into a new source of export revenue.

The company was a subsidiary of BHP until the mid-1980s. Chief Executive, Wilton Ainsworth, describes its fortunes before then: 'Comsteel had performed fairly well during the sixties and seventies but, entering the eighties, with reductions to tariff barriers, quite rapidly escalating labour costs, we were faced with diminishing profit. In fact, in the early eighties, Comsteel generated trading losses, so that, about the time the steel industry came under very close review [by the Federal Government], Comsteel was not performing very well at all.'

Under ANI, Ainsworth had the job of turning that performance around. He began a long process of negotiating change with the metal trades unions. There was much to change both in terms of work practices and the size of the workforce. One plant, for example, did not operate from midnight to dawn. But workers were still assigned to be there every night during those hours. With no work to do, they slept. A foreman sacked one of them once—not for sleeping as such but for sleeping away from his lathe; but even he was reinstated after a dispute between union and management.

Award restructuring took place gradually through 1988 and 1989 and such perks as 'the sleeping shift' as the workers called it, disappeared. 'Restructuring here is more advanced than in most other parts of manufacturing industry,' Ainsworth says.

He says that union officials and employees also understood that the workforce had to be reduced and, from 2000 at the time of the ANI takeover, it has now been cut to about 1000. 'We haven't retrenched those 1000 people that no longer work here,' Ainsworth explains. 'Over that period, there are retirements, people go to other positions, people change their employment naturally all the time. So that it hasn't been a painful reduction because it's taken place over five years. And we'll continue to reduce the workforce here because everything we do is aimed at better productivity.' Of those who remain, he says: 'They'll be more effectively employed, they'll be employed in more satisfying roles, the jobs are more interesting, and Comsteel is doing much more to retrain and develop skills within people.'

But Comsteel shows that workplace reform involves far more than changing the workforce. It also means improving management and investing in modern equipment. Comsteel needed both.

'Much of the plant was 40 to 50 years old and it was quite labour intensive and, in changing that, there's been a large amount of capital investment made in the plant,' Ainsworth says. 'We commenced that process in the steel plant because all our end products are produced from steel that's melted at Comsteel from scrap . . . That involved installation of a continuous caster—an investment of around 10 million—and has been followed by a new 50 tonne ultra high-power arc furnace. That arc furnace, together with a ladle refining furnace, cost us in the order of $20 million and . . . we now have productivity figures similar to plants overseas. We have state-of-the-art steel-making for both basic and special alloy steels, so that we're now in a position to produce our range of products from very efficient low-cost feedstock. The productivity figures in that area are quite amazing. The productivity today is almost three times what it was three years ago. That gives you some idea of the streamlining in that area.'

Comsteel has several end products: steel grinding balls for crushing ore; railway wheels and axles; large forgings, including deep-hardened rolls for rolling mills; and steel rolled in its own rolling mills. The company decided to concentrate capital investment on those sections which would benefit from it the most and generate a commensurate return. It has so far spent $2.5 million on a new lathe for rolls and $9 million on a new grinding ball plant. The total new investment since the ANI takeover has therefore been $41.5 million and further spending is likely.

The new grinding ball plant is particularly significant. Although this is a relatively low value-added activity, it accounts for 50 per cent of the company's steel-making and has growing export potential. Around 30 per cent of its output already goes overseas. The new plant replaced two old production units, one of which was second-hand when it was installed 20 years ago. 'The new ball plant is capable of producing around 100 000 tonnes a year which is double the capacity of our two older plants,' Ainsworth says.

Perhaps the most dramatic change introduced since the ANI takeover has been in the area of management practices 'During the early period of the restructuring we devoted considerable effort to strategic analysis of the company' position,' Ainsworth says. 'It became apparent that we didn' have much flexibility in respect to changing our products– that we had to develop particular strategies for each of th major products that we were committed to and, in pursuin those strategy reviews, we came to the conclusion that som of the products could only be viable for Comsteel if we move into export markets in a much more significant way . .

'However, in the early eighties, the company w

structured centrally and there was little focus on the individual product groups. So one of the major moves has been to split the company up into business units so that we could apply greater focus to the individual product groups, the market opportunities, and the plant capacity to be efficient in manufacturing those particular products.'

When the the new grinding ball plant was coming into full production in 1989, for example, a business unit meeting—with personnel ranging from supervisors from the shopfloor to the business unit manager—was held every morning. Production rates and quality were discussed and then marketing developments described. All of this ensured that those leading the business unit were in command of the totality of its production and distribution.

Comsteel has also trimmed the number of positions for staff—as distinct from shopfloor employees—in line with its overall workforce reductions. 'The staff levels here today are very close to half the staff levels that existed in the early eighties,' Ainsworth says. 'At the same time, the company is producing and selling something like 50 per cent more than it did in the early eighties and it's selling more product on overseas markets, so there is greater involvement of management personnel in supporting that sort of marketing effort. It's fairly evident in doing that that spans of responsibility have had to be greatly enlarged in the management area and, in fact, business unit managers now are expected to function largely as general managers in their own right.'

The new combination of leaner, more functionally organised management, modernised plant and workforce restructuring has paid off for Comsteel: after several traumatic years, it is now in the black.

Media reporting of industrial relations in Australia tends to be dominated by stories of industrial disputes and, particularly in the era of the Hawke Government's wages accord', pay claims. While there is no doubting their importance, concentration upon them has tended to obscure other vital developments with less headline-grabbing impact: productivity; training; modernisation; award restructuring;

and so on. Yet, if changes are not made in these less glamorous areas, industrial peace and wage restraint will not by themselves transform the fate of our manufacturing industry and enable it to compete internationally.

And changes are starting to happen. Industrial Relations Minister Peter Morris compares Australia's performance with other countries and says: 'We're ahead of some; we're behind others. But, as far as Australia's concerned, we need to go faster.'

He describes workplace reform as 'a gigantic task' and adds: 'The only way that we'll be able to maintain job security in this country and continue to add new jobs . . . is by becoming world class in our industry—world class meaning world competitive. And that means a continuing process of change . . . become more productive, become more efficient, make work more interesting and satisfying, give people proper training and give people an opportunity to get ahead. Now that is the only way. There is no future for manufacturing industry other than that way.'

6 The Last
Few Metres

IF Australia is to be export competitive, it must be able to transport its products as cheaply and dependably as possible. The biggest single obstacle to this is the Australian waterfront. Those last few metres of Australia are adding too much to the cost of our exports. More importantly, the journey across them is unreliable. A delay in Sydney's Port Botany or in the Port of Melbourne can cause disenchantment among distributors in the United States or cancelled orders in Japan.

Freight and transport questions have always been serious matters for Australian exporters. We have long and thin lines of shipping to foreign markets, particularly the dominant northern hemisphere markets, and overseas groups own most of the ships. This domination has sometimes led to onerous pricing arrangements for exporters. But an international shipping glut in the 1980s has minimised, even reversed, these effects. And the Federal Government has legislated to make shipping group arrangements more subject to scrutiny.

As airline services between Australia and the rest of the world have improved, our reliance on ships has lessened. For manufacturers of high value-added, lightweight, low-volume products, air freight has become an affordable and quicker alternative. It has also created new export opportunities for perishables, such as horticultural and food products. The most prized tuna can leave, say, the New South Wales fishing town of Bega one day and be sold in the Tokyo markets for sashimi the next.

But ships still transport the vast majority of our exports.

And one aspect of shipping has remained a major matter of concern for exporters: the waterfront, or to use a more pedantic but accurate term, shore-based services. A report to the Inter-State Commission (ISC) by the Association of Australian Port and Marine Authorities in July 1988 summed up the situation: 'It is readily apparent that the shore-based shipping operation is inefficient and is afflicted by a vast range of well-entrenched problems which have led to a lack of service reliability, low productivity and high cost for our vital export industries.'

Australia lags far behind the performance of leading overseas ports. Major European container terminals turn ships around in as little as 12 hours. And, once cargo is unloaded, it moves swiftly off the wharves and on to its destination. In one West German terminal, the operators pay a penalty if they delay a truck for more than 10 minutes.

The contrast with Australia is stark. In October 1989, the Australia to Europe Shipping Conference announced the imposition of a 'congestion' surcharge of $200 on every container shipped in or out of Sydney. It put the blame for the surcharge on the fact that, on average, vessels are delayed for two days every time they load or unload at Sydney although the delays at times stretch to two weeks.

The conference, which represents major owners of ships on the Australia–Europe run, estimated that the delays had cost them $16 million in the first nine months of 1989. said it could no longer shoulder the burden of subsidising importers and exporters for the hold-ups. The *Australian* newspaper said the surcharge would cost the shipping line customers at least $30 million in a full year.

The Australian waterfront is like the rest of our workplaces: its problems do not result from a single cause. And an Importer/Exporter Panel which reported to the Inter State Commission in 1988 made an important distinction between the symptoms of those problems and the underlying diseases when it found: 'Entrenched symptoms, such inefficient work and management practices, must be dealt with properly, as they have an independent life; however a more vital task is to tackle the causes that sustain them.

One thing this means is that—contrary to what may

people do—you cannot just blame the wharfies whenever there are delays and disruption. In fact, it is worth emphasising that many people other than those we call wharfies, that is, members of the Waterside Workers Federation, work on the waterfront. They constitute lttle more than one-fifth of the workforce; 5400 out of 26 000. The rest are clerks, storemen and packers, drivers, tugmen and others.

In line with other workplaces, we must not look only at employees when assessing problems. Management, in this case, port authorities, stevedoring companies and shippers themselves, has made its contribution. So has the working environment—the ports and their facilities.

How well all of these elements function has long been a subject of special attention. Horst Rilk, Australian managing director of the Columbus Line, points out that there have been 24 inquiries into the waterfront since Australia was federated in 1901. Given the continued complaints, they have had an abysmal success rate.

Tas Bull, the Federal secretary of the Waterside Workers Federation, has a strong wariness of inquiries: 'I'd be more interested in bringing about what these days seem to be called attitudinal changes in the workforce, rather than concentrating on reassembling—for about the umpteenth time in the period I've been in the industry—what I describe as the "Leggo pieces". There's too much attention to changing the industry's structures and too little attention to how you get people to adopt different attitudes.'

But the latest inquiry holds out some real promise of change. The Inter-State Commission spent more than two years examining the Australian waterfront before reporting in March 1989. The result is the most far-reaching analysis of the problems so far undertaken.

The question remains as to how speedily reforms can be introduced. Australia has a long way to go before it even approaches the efficiency of major overseas ports.

Hamburg has been a port for eight centuries. Traditionally, its position well upstream from the North Sea was its advantage: the deep estuary of the River Elbe protected it from predatory neighbours. Now, its location is a commercial liability: it is eight hours slow and precise steaming from the sea. Every time a ship goes there, it is adding 16 hours to its journey as it plies up and then down the river.

Rotterdam and other ports with more direct access to the North Sea are not far away. Competition between the ports is fierce. So Hamburg has to make up for its natural disadvantages with man-made efficiencies. And it does just that.

A good example is the Unikai Container Terminal. It offers guarantees of performance. It has achieved a turnaround rate that, by Australian standards, is impossible. If a truck is delayed more than 10 minutes, the terminal pays the owner a penalty. It guarantees to handle 40 containers an hour. Any less, and it pays a penalty to the shipowner. Seldom is either penalty paid.

The aim is to have ships in and out in 12 hours, with 700 containers handled. And handled does not mean just dumped on the wharf. The containers are put on to transport which immediately whisks them away from the terminal. The terminal management regards getting containers on and off ships as relatively easy but devotes much thought and planning to getting them to and from the terminal.

Labour in Hamburg is expensive. West Germany has generous social benefits, including health and pension allowances, which almost double the wages bill. This has spurred rapid advances in mechanisation. The Unikai terminal is so automated that it could switch to operating virtually without people. The workforce has already been reduced by three-quarters: only 150 people operate the terminal and that includes managers, as well as workers.

Those who choose union membership—about 7 out of 10—belong to one national union which negotiates three to five-year contracts with employers. The contracts contain a no-strikes guarantee. It is 10 years since the last strike which management says was its own fault for leaving new contract negotiations until the last minute.

From the perspective of Hamburg, the Australian waterfront looks bad. It is of real interest there because the German port is the headquarters for two of the biggest shipping lines on the Australian run—Hapag Lloyd and Columbus. Hapag Lloyd director Peter Kulenkampff-Boedecker told a shipping conference in Australia in 1988 that, in the jumble of organisations, associations, committees, governments and unions, he could not see that anyone was doing anything much for improvements.

A year later, in an interview in Hamburg, he was a little more diplomatic: 'We need to see an improvement because, while we are accustomed to ups and downs, I think we are due for an up now.' But his summing up of Australia's standing remained unflattering. Australian ports cost twice as much for half the productivity when compared with other 'normal standard' world ports. He adds: 'Where has Australia gone wrong? I think Australia has just probably missed chances to improve.'

On a visit to Sydney in 1989, Herman van Leeuwen, a container terminal executive from Rotterdam, also compared Australian productivity unfavourably with Dutch. He estimated it is less than half of the productivity of his home port. Could European ports afford such a performance? 'In Rotterdam, for instance, no, absolutely not,' he says. 'It would] kill us within five years and bring us back to the Third World.'

After looking them over, he describes new container facilities in Port Botany, Sydney, as 'excellent'. So he wonders whether the difference in productivity is more a matter of cultural or social background. He also suggests that competition—or the lack of it—is a major explanation. Competitors of Rotterdam are basically Antwerp, Zeebrugge [Belgium], Le Havre [France], Hamburg, Bremen [West Germany], Felixstowe [UK],' he says. 'So we have a lot of competitors in, let's say, a circle of about 200 to 250 kilometres round Rotterdam.'

In contrast, great distances separate major Australian ports and they therefore have more of a monopoly on traffic to and from their respective hinterlands. This fact of geography forced the Inter-State Commission to look for ways to increase competition within, rather than between, our ports. But, even here, there are problems. The Commission pointed out that, compared to the 1950s when there were numerous operators: 'Almost all stevedoring is now performed by four company groups.'

It went on: 'The Commission considers that the future role of port authorities is particularly important in promoting competition and regulating monopolies. There is no possibility of new stevedoring companies operating if they cannot gain access to facilities. Where there is capacity for more operators, incentives can be provided to attract new companies without too great a loss in efficiency. Some of the extreme effects of monopolies can be controlled by including appropriate performance and pricing requirements in leases.'

There is another obvious geographical contrast between Australian and European ports: places like Rotterdam are less than 24 hours from almost any Western European destination. In other words, they service one of the richest markets in the world, concentrated in a relatively small area. This inevitably means high volumes of traffic which, in turn, justify capital expenditure to get the very best facilities

Tas Bull, of the Waterside Workers Federation, supports this view: 'There are economies of scale which are possible in places like Rotterdam. They are just developing a new terminal for one customer alone. That single client American Sealand, will in fact handle as many containers on its ships alone through the one part of the port of Rotterdam as we handle in the whole of Australia.' Bull points out that technology also combines with good management: 'In Rotterdam, I have observed myself each cycle of the crane carries a container in and out of the ship. In Australia, for reasons of organisation and technology the ship is either loading or discharging, not both simultaneously.'

The services that feed into a port are also important Rotterdam's proximity to its markets is enhanced because the port is where four great transport systems of Europe converge: trucks, trains, river barges and ships. Part of its magic, by Australian standards, is the way in which the systems are integrated. So a ship will arrive in the morning and head back to sea that night, with its loading and unloading completed. But it remains true that it has

THE LAST FEW METRES 117

perform so well: otherwise the trade will go elsewhere.

Another port whose efficiency is driven by competition is Tacoma, in the American state of Washington. Of its two rivals for shipping on the West Coast, one of them—Seattle—is only a short boat ride away along Puget Sound. (The other rival is Long Beach, further south in California.) John J. Terpstra, executive director of the Port of Tacoma Commission, boasts that it is the fastest growing port on the West Coast. Its container traffic, for example, has increased by 421 per cent in five years. He estimates that, before long, Tacoma and Seattle together will handle more containers than New York–New Jersey—a reflection of the growing importance of Pacific Rim trade.

Tacoma's turnaround of each container ship is 24 to 36 hours. It also offers other advantages: good highway and rail connections; plenty of land for warehouse facilities; and excellent industrial relations. According to Terpstra, Tacoma's longshoremen 'sometimes almost act a little like management'. He adds: 'We're a team. We always have been, as a tradition at this port . . . We have virtually no work stoppages. We have regular contacts and candid, open discussions between management and labour. We meet monthly between our stevedores and our longshore union and management of the port to resolve problems. The longshoremen regularly state that they know that this cargo doesn't have to come here and, by them being able to keep it here, gives them jobs, too.'

The longshoremen's co-operation is well rewarded. Their average salary is about $US50 000 a year. Crane drivers do even better with annual earnings of around $US80 000. But they are not well paid at the expense of cost-efficient operation. 'We at the port operate like a business,' Terpstra says. 'We look at our bottom line, we look at our profit and we look at our ability to provide to our customers a better facility, a better service, at a proper price.'

Across the Pacific from Tacoma, Hong Kong works cargo as fast as anywhere—and more of it: more containers go through Hong Kong than through any other port in the world. Yet the harbour has some considerable disadvantages. With its crowded hinterland, queues of trucks feeding into the wharves can stretch for kilometres. And there's a shortage of wharf space, so ships unload on to lighters, large barges which shuttle cargo ashore.

For all that, shippers say Hong Kong is faster and cheaper than the most modern Australian ports. It costs $US50 less to unload a container in Hong Kong than it does in Australia. And a Hong Kong visit is $US50 000 cheaper in ship time than a stay in one of our ports.

Only the driest of economists or most brutal of business people would suggest that Australians should adopt the social and industrial conditions which prevail in Hong Kong and which contribute to its superior waterfront performance. But we must acknowledge that the Australian waterfront is one more impediment to our competitiveness as international traders.

Don Hanson has been a waterside worker on the Sydney wharves for about 40 years and he is tired of the way outsiders blame his workmates and him for anything that goes wrong. 'We've been crucified by the media for years and years,' he says. He has a special contempt for talk-back radio commentators: 'They seem to put their mouth into gear before they do their homework.' A shipping delay will be blamed on the wharfies even if it is caused by a machine breakdown.

Of the cranes and other equipment on the wharves, he says: 'I think Captain Cook brought them out. And then they try to tell us we can't compete with the people overseas and that's true because [of] their technology compared with what we've got here; it's just laughable.'

He points to organisational problems: 'If this wharf full of containers, they'll give the truck people three days to pick them up. But they'll leave them here for two days. They build up because they're getting free storage. And the third day [the truck queue] will be a mile long.' That, too, is blamed on the wharfies. 'I'm sick of getting crucified the media,' he says. 'I've put up with it for 40 years. You can't even convince your own mate in the pub about it.

Outside Swanson Dock, one of the busiest wharves in the Port of Melbourne, two truckies are caught in a long queue of vehicles—a common occurrence. 'I started yesterday morning at 4 o'clock,' one says. 'I delivered one [container load] in and I took one out and I got finished at 10 o'clock last night. That's generally pretty well average for most of the blokes around here, too.' His mate joins in: 'That's why we can't export nothing because everybody's just sitting around waiting to get in there.'

Don Hanson and the truckies give just a couple of indications that the faults in Australia's shore-based services are multiple. Unnecessary expense and delays can affect export cargo on its way to the wharves, on the wharves and on ships as they head out to sea.

An early stage of that journey is the container depot. If an Australian exporter is dispatching goods which are less than a full container load—LCL, in the industry jargon—the goods must be packed into a container at a Customs-approved depot. For historical reasons, depots handling trans-Tasman trade are manned by members of the Transport Workers Union, while depots handling other international trade are manned jointly by members of the Waterside Workers Federation and the Storemen and Packers Union.

A report to the Inter-State Commission in 1988 found that, in 1988, it cost an estimated $600 to pack or unpack a container at an international depot but only $250 for packing and $300 for unpacking the same size of container at a trans-Tasman depot. 'Cargo throughput was also much quicker in the trans-Tasman depots,' the report said. 'These two types of depots operate under different industrial conditions—the contribution of labour costs was 73 per cent in the waterfront depots and 35 per cent in the trans-Tasman depots.'

Because of long-standing industrial agreements, trans-Tasman depots are not allowed to handle other international cargo, even when the international depots are overloaded. So there is no way round the higher charges for LCL exports going anywhere other than New Zealand.

Overseas comparisons are quite alarming. The International Forwarders Association of Australia told the ISC: 'We can get containers unpacked for $175 in the USA. In Hong Kong we pack or unpack containers for the

equivalent of about $200 per 20-foot container.' The New
South Wales State Chamber of Commerce and Industry gave
evidence that the cost of unpacking a non-refrigerated LCL
container in the international depots could go as high as
$1290, 'while the comparative cost to unpack that same
container in Hamburg is $187 on current exchange rates.'

The ISC reported a lack of competition between container
depot operators. In Sydney, for example, there were 'ten times
the number of air freight depots to handle a fraction of the
freight handled by the much smaller number of sea freight
container depots'.

As cargo approaches the wharves, there are the problems
signalled by the Melbourne truckies. A Waterfront Industry
Committee, appointed by the ISC, reported average figures
on truck delays which were very much lower than those
suggested by the truckies. Average waiting time in Melbourne
had dropped from two hours to one hour over a two-year
period. But the ISC reported 'a considerable amount of
evidence on the lack of appropriate procedures for road and
rail access to ports'. It quoted the Australian Shippers
Council as saying: 'Inefficiencies in the interface between
land transport and waterfront operations are well
documented and generally persist despite the efforts of
few operators to overcome them.'

Captain Peter McGovern, Deputy Principal of the
Australian Maritime College, who has made a special study
of port facilities internationally, says that part of the problem
in a port such as Melbourne is that the waterfront work
three shifts a day, seven days a week, while the road haulage
industry does not. Many trucking companies operate for only
five days a week. That can turn the roads approaching
terminals and wharves into bedlam on Fridays as operators
try to finish off their deliveries for the week.

'In really bad, congested conditions—conditions where
there's no discipline on the part of the shippers, where there
no discipline on the part of the truck operators, where the
terminal is suffering from some sort of congestion or perhaps
mechanical breakdown—delays can extend into perhaps
full working day,' McGovern says. 'In some cases, the truck
operators are paid on [the basis of] time and therefore you

can see that that's a real problem because, the longer the container sits on the back of the truck, the more money the truck earns.'

The next phase sees cargo go on to a wharf. If it is containerised, it will be stacked in readiness for loading on to a ship. A problem for the Australian waterfront is the high cost of the best equipment for stacking and moving containers around. Captain McGovern points out that a straddle carrier—which looms over a container like a giant grasshopper, picks it up and then moves off with it—is worth more than $1 million and a heavy fork-lift truck about $700 000. The higher the turnover of a port, the more equipment of this kind is justified. So it is inevitable that busy ports overseas are better equipped than lower-turnover Australian ports.

When the time comes to lift the cargo on to a ship, mechanisation can again affect performance but only be improved expensively: some of the cranes used are worth several million dollars each, according to McGovern. It is his part of the operation which has been most often criticised in Australia for its slowness. 'Some work which related the rates at which [crane] lifts are carried out in Australia to the rates at which lifts are carried out in New Zealand and Europe indicated that, on some occasions, there's only half the productivity in Australia that one might expect in Europe,' he says.

While mechanisation might have some role in explaining this difference, McGovern suggests it 'in part at least can be sheeted back to work practices'. At the same time, this can be a reflection of 'our Australian lifestyle such that the productivity we have is one that suits not only the people that work on the wharf but all the rest [of Australians].'

And so we come to the people who work on the wharves. There is a strong argument that problems start with the structures in which they work. The concentration of ownership of stevedoring companies in Australia has been mentioned earlier in this chapter. The University of Wollongong's Centre for Transport Policy Analysis reported to the ISC on 'a highly concentrated industry with a history of comfortable co-existence and customers willing to pay premiums to guarantee uninterrupted service'—an industry which, even when under pressure, 'accepts the underlying cost structure as given'. Freely translated, this can mean that a stevedoring company will bow to union pressure for a concession involving easier work practices or better pay on the assumption that it can pass any extra costs on to an affected shipowner because his main interest will be in keeping his fleet moving quickly in and out of port.

That argument gains strength when a couple of estimates by Columbus Line's Horst Rilk are taken into account: that it costs about $30 000 a day to run a ship; and that, if a company's ships are making 50 voyages to Australia a year a delay of three days on every trip would cost it the equivalent of two of those voyages.

Sweetheart deals have been the modern response to the tense industrial world of the waterfront. In earlier days, the tension was resolved more brutally. Many wharfies retain a strong awareness of the days when this was epitomised by the 'Hungry Mile' a stretch of the inner-Sydney waterfront where many men would jostle and plead for a few casual day-labouring jobs.

Tas Bull, who has spent his working life at sea or on the wharves, can remember much tougher times in the past. 'We only had permanent employment introduced to the industry in '67 and, as recently as [1977], the extension of it across all of our workforce. We're probably the last group in this country to get sick leave, annual leave, long-service leave. In the period leading up to the establishment of those conditions this was a turbulent industry and the dispute levels were very high. Today, it is less than one per cent of the time worked and I think that compares favourably with many other sectors of industry that it is reasonable to compare us with, such as mining, building and so on.

Bull is correct in saying that industrial disputes have declined. He is also correct in saying that waterfront disputation compares favourably with the mining and construction industries. But those industries have bad—in some cases, appalling—industrial records by Australian standards. The Inter-State Commission compiled figures compare working days lost for each thousand employees

Australian industry from 1979 to 1987. Using 1987 as a sample, this shows that coalminers lost 8902 days per thousand employees—by far the worst group. Then came stevedoring employees with 1201 lost days, followed by employees in mining (other than coalmining) with 1069 lost days. After them were construction industry workers (773 lost days). So, by Bull's test, waterside employees were much less strike-prone than coalminers, a little bit worse than other miners and decidedly worse than construction workers.

But further comparisons are far less flattering. Metal production, machinery and equipment employees lost 479 days and those in other manufacturing industry only 305 days. So the waterfront employees' industrial record was 2.5 to 4 times worse than those groups. And, if the number of days lost per thousand employees is averaged out across all industries, it amounted to only 223 days. In other words, the stevedoring disputation rate was more than five times worse than the average for all Australian workers.

The National Farmers Federation, which has become the most savage right-wing critic of the Waterside Workers Federation, submitted to the Inter-State Commission that 'Data collected by BIMCO, the international strike insurance club, consistently reveal that Australia has the worst industrial relations record affecting shipping of all its members.'

Pay and working conditions are not the only causes of Australian waterfront industrial disputes. This probably reflects the fact that waterside workers, for example, are now quite well paid, compared to other workers. Average earnings for registered regular waterside workers in 1986–87 were $31 468; the all-industry average was $23 670. Other concerns lay behind many strikes. The ISC found that, in the 10 years to 1986–87, political issues accounted for 15 per cent of waterfront strikes; trade union matters—including demarcation, actions supporting other unions and over the use of non-union labour—were responsible for 30 per cent of stoppages.

So, while long-time wharfie, Don Hanson, is right to defend his workmates against getting the blame for all of Australia's waterfront problems, they still contribute to them.

Some of that contribution has nothing to do with strikes and, indeed, cannot be a subject of blame. An example are the problems of the ageing and fitness of waterside workers. The ISC reported in 1988 that the average age of full-time wharfies was 50 and that 33 per cent of them were 55 or over. This is markedly out of kilter with the overall Australian workforce and matters significantly in an industry which involves physical labour.

About 14 per cent of wharfies also had at least one disability exemption. 'This means these workers may be exempt from lifting, working on board ships or operating particular type of equipment,' the ISC explained. Appropriately, the Commission proposed funding arrangements to allow many older and unfit wharfies to retire so the workforce could be rejuvenated.

Inadequate training and poor motivation also hinder performance. Tas Bull points out that his members get only five weeks training, compared to six months for Swedish waterside workers. And there is not very much to strive for when there is only about a $25 difference between the lowest and highest paid operational wharfie.

In moving cargo on to and across Australian wharves not all the problems are human or mechanical. Another difficulty involves paper—mountains of it—and other means of communication. The ISC set up a National Communications Working Party to look at it. It reported 'Participants in the transport and handling chain use many different means of communication . . . A small army of messengers is employed couriering documents around the ports, and information about shipping and cargo availability is obtained from a daily newspaper or by countless telephone calls, telexes and facsimiles. Late receipt of documents and inaccurate documentation contribute to truck delays on the waterfront, adding to importers' and exporters' costs. The communications maze is a major factor in the opaqueness of the transport and handling system, both for consumers (importers and exporters) and participants in the system itself . . . Overseas experience indicates that between 3.5 and 7 per cent of transport costs can be saved by adopting modern electronic communications systems.'

The working party brought interested parties together to form a management company which is currently organising an electronic data interchange (EDI) network. And the Australian Customs Service has already installed a new computerised documentation system.

Keeping track of cargo and simplifying documentation is not important simply as a cost-saving exercise for transport operators. It is also vital to exporters in other ways. One document, the bill of lading, is especially so: many international transactions are completed at the point at which this is handed over to an exporter by a shipping company's representative. Ownership of goods is often transferred from the exporter to the overseas buyer then. A bill of lading can be used to activate letters of credit and otherwise to enable the exporter to be paid.

And so the exporter's goods are finally aboard ship, the mooring ropes are cast off and everything seems set for plain sailing. Not necessarily, since it remains for the ship to be guided out of the harbour to the open sea and there are complaints about this stage of export process, too.

The ISC received criticisms of tug services in Australian ports on grounds including lack of competition and high concentration of ownership, high costs, excessive crewing and over-servicing. ISC studies suggest that some problems are unavoidable because of market size, among other reasons. But a study by the Federal Bureau of Transport and Communications Economics presents a strong case for a reduction in the size of tug crews. Cutting crew numbers to four from their present levels of around five or six would save the shipping industry $13 million a year and could reduce towage charges between 5 and 25 per cent, the bureau found.

The latest attempt to unravel the Australian waterfront's complex tale of woe began when the Federal Government asked the Inter-State Commission to conduct an inquiry in December 1986. Between then and the presentation of its conclusions and recommendations in March 1989, it laboured mightily, as the statistics demonstrate: 147 submissions, 4480 pages of transcript, investigation of 200 separate issues, commissioning of 10 consultancy studies and other special reports.

The Inter-State Commission, on the surface, was a strange organisation to conduct the waterfront inquiry. Its existence is prescribed in the Australian Constitution and, accordingly, it is an organ of independent standing alongside the Federal Parliament, the Executive Council and the High Court. But, since Federation, that existence has been theoretical for far longer than it has been actual.

Section 101 of the Constitution provides: 'There shall be an Inter-State Commission, with such powers of adjudication and administration as the Parliament deems necessary for the execution and maintenance, within the Commonwealth of the provisions of the Constitution relating to trade and commerce, and of all laws made thereunder.' Under Section 98, this power is specifically extended to cover 'navigation and shipping, and . . . railways the property of any State'

Intended to allay some of the last State fears about Federation, it had no immediate life and then only a short one: it was not until 1913 that a Commission of three was appointed; it had effectively lapsed by 1920. It was to lie undisturbed until the 1970s.

Then, with its unrealised legal potential, it presented just the sort of opportunity that delighted the politician-lawyer Gough Whitlam. He could enjoy the resurrection of such an institution in much the same way that a business magnate might revel in the revitalising of an under-utilised asset after a company takeover. The Senate, however, watered down his more ambitious proposals and, he complained in *The Whitlam Government: 1972–75*, 'confined the Commission activities to the investigation of transport-related matters and then only upon the direction of the Minister'.

The Bill did not receive Royal assent until 27 October 1975—15 days before Whitlam's dismissal by Sir John Kerr. It took the re-election of another Labor Government in 198 for it to be brought back to life for the first time in more than 60 years. In March 1984, this old sop to pre-Federation fears staggered to its feet. Whatever the uncertainties of its background, once it was up and running, it had some definite advantages—as it boasted in a recent annual report: 'The

Commission has Royal Commission-type powers, and this places it in a unique position to assess national transport issues.'

By 1986, it was ready to undertake the waterfront inquiry. In the following year, E. W. A. (Ted) Butcher, who, starting in his native United Kingdom, had many years of experience in the transport industry, became president of the Commission. The two other members were G. K. R. Reid, a former director of the Federal Bureau of Transport Economics, and Professor M. Coper, Associate Professor of Law at the University of New South Wales.

The waterfront had changed greatly in the two decades before the Commission's inquiry. In June 1989, Ralph Willis, Minister for Transport and Communications in the Hawke Government, gave this description of the most important development affecting stevedoring: 'Twenty years ago, containerisation was introduced to Australian ports. It fundamentally changed the face of the waterfront. The number of cargo-handling waterside workers has reduced from 21 000 in the years before containerisation to a little over 5000 now. Between 1965 and 1985, the amount of non-bulk cargo handled by each waterside worker increased from 1000 tonnes to over 5000 tonnes a year.'

But he warned against deriving too much pleasure from these figures: 'Despite these larger increases in labour productivity, we haven't kept pace with our overseas competitors.' The Australian waterfront industry had remained grossly inefficient'. In other words, it was the technological change itself—containerisation—which had brought the rises in productivity, not improvements in work and management practices.

In the stevedoring sector alone, the ISC had before it a study by the University of Wollongong's Centre for Transport Policy Analysis which estimated that an overall productivity improvement of 60 per cent was possible. 'This, in turn, implies direct labour cost savings of nearly 35 per cent,' the ISC reported.

In 1989, the ISC proposed a package of reforms with a primary objective: 'to eliminate waterfront-related transport impediments to Australia's trade and to achieve reliable, cost-effective transport for exporters and importers'. While its proposals aroused some criticism from the interested parties, the bulk of them were adopted by the Federal Government. One tangible result has been the establishment of the Waterfront Industry Reform Authority to run for three years. Its name makes clear its purpose and function.

The ISC left no doubt that major reform is needed. It included these elements in a summary of 'the classic symptoms of an imperfect market' to be found on the waterfront: ineffective management; poor workforce training and career arrangements; introspective industrial attitudes; poor response to user needs; poor information flows to users and between links in the transport chain; lack of supply and demand balance, often reflected in congestion and queues or in under-utilisation of expensive facilities; diffusion of governmental responsibility; and abuse of monopoly power, reflected particularly in port authority pricing and investment policies.

It took a look back over its shoulder at the poor results from earlier inquiries when it added to this list: 'a tendency for matters to improve considerably while they are under investigation but to lapse once the pressure is removed.' The summary continued: 'To this litany can be added high costs, endemic unreliability, a high level of disputation, inappropriate manning levels and work practices, poor discipline, poor motivation throughout the industry, and a pervasive lack of competition.'

No one knows just how high the cost of this comprehensive muddle is. In its submissions to the ISC, the Association of Australian Port and Marine Authorities asserted that 'excess shore-based direct and indirect shipping costs totalled $1028 million in 1986–87'. The ISC itself estimated that the overall benefit of the kind of micro-economic reform it proposed for the waterfront 'will be at least $620 million per annum when the plan is fully implemented'. If the economy-wide effects of waterside inefficiency could be accurately computed, there seems little doubt that this estimate would be shown to be very conservative.

As has been noted earlier in this chapter, the Inter-State Commission report and the Hawke Government's response are the latest in a long line of attempts to improve the Australian waterfront. There is a new urgency about the task because of the importance of those last few metres of Australia to our export drive. It will require a new and unusual spirit of co-operation in an industry more used to disputes or, when there is agreement, self-serving advantage.

As hopeful a sign as any is the reaction to the ISC report by Tas Bull, of the Waterside Workers Federation: 'Our members have to understand the importance of this particular industry and lift their game as each other sector in Australia is being asked to do . . . I think [the ISC] has been an important catalyst to cause everyone, including the members of my own union, to re-examine their position.'

7 Starting Out

THROUGHOUT this book have been stories of export achievement, of Australians who have developed good products at home and then created or seized opportunities to market them to the world. But add them all up and there are simply not enough of them. And put a financial value on their exported goods and what a number of them earn would amount to pin money by international standards. Our growing current account deficit, which gives us some measure of the size and success of our overseas trading, tells us that.

If Australia was a person with a cheque account, we would be standing red-faced in front of our bank manager. The ledgers would reveal that we are spending more than we are earning, that we have already borrowed more than we should and that we have even been selling off some major assets to pay for our profligacy.

In fact, Australia is a collection of people with bank accounts which are starting to reflect the underlying problems of our trading position as a nation. As individuals the balance between what we are earning and what we are paying is changing, too. A Bureau of Statistics survey showed that, in 1988–89, average household expenditure in Australia was $506.87 a week—while the average weekly wage for Australians in May 1989 was $5.77 less than that. In 1984 a similar survey found that average weekly household expenditure was $361.84 while the average gross household income was $453.60.

It is little wonder that Laurie Carmichael warns us that our living standards are seriously threatened by long-term problems. That is why he can find common ground with people on the other side of the political fence—industry leaders such as John Ralph of CRA, who says: 'The first thing to be communicated is that it really is a crisis and we therefore have to look at radical solutions to fix it.'

Ralph goes on: 'We have been making some improvements but we're not moving fast enough. We have to understand that it's not enough comparing where we are today with where we were three or four years ago—but recognising that, during that three or four years, our competitors have also improved their performance.'

The improvement needs to happen at the start of the export process—in the workplace—and carry through to the point of departure—the waterfront—and beyond into the international marketplace itself. And the improvements have to be real rather than illusory.

An example of the difficulty of distinguishing between apparent and actual betterment applies to the Australian workplace. As discussed in chapter 5, one of Australia's great needs in this area is for plant modernisation. There has therefore been a necessary tolerance towards imports of machinery and equipment to further that process. But there is a considerable question mark over just what proportion of our increased imports have had this productive purpose.

In the *Australian Financial Review* in September 1989, economist David Clark took his questioning beyond what has already happened:

> Hopefully, investment in machinery and equipment will continue to rise over 1990. Surveys of investment intentions suggest that it will—although intentions can change, especially in an era of high interest rates. Without much more new machinery and equipment we have no chance of achieving significant import replacement and/or a further expansion in our manufactured exports. However, most of the improvement promised for 1990 will also go into the non-traded goods sector— into data processing equipment for the tourist industry and the finance sector—rather than into factories making import-replacing goods or goods for export.

At the other end of the export process, our manufacturers have to think strategically about our markets. It is obvious that Australia's days of imperial dependence are a long way in the past. The United Kingdom in 1986-87 took just over 4 per cent of our merchandise exports. While that makes it a significant individual market—and, in AUSTRADE's estimation, one that is even likely to grow slightly by the early 1990s—it is greatly overshadowed by markets with which we have fewer long-standing ties.

The countries which are in, or border, the Pacific should dominate our export consciousness. If we include North and South Asia, North America, Oceania and the Pacific nations of South America in this group, it already accounts for three-quarters of our exports. North Asia alone—Japan, China, Korea, Taiwan and Hong Kong—took about 44 per cent of our exports in 1986-87 and AUSTRADE expects this to grow by several percentage points by the early 1990s.

This is not to say that we should ignore the rest of the world. Western Europe is an important market. And, as we have seen, Eastern Europe offers some very interesting prospects as it undergoes extraordinary political, social and economic change.

But we have entered the era of the global economy and competition in every market is intense. We have to assume that no one owes us any favours, that we must fight hard to find new markets and fight just as hard to hang on to existing ones.

For Australian manufacturers, this means new attitudes, new pressures, a whole new culture—an export culture. Sir Peter Abeles makes the point that, in fact, this change involves more than our business people. 'The attitudes have to change at all levels,' he says. 'I see signs that, particularly in the last 10 years, there is a change but . . . [for] a country which has been used to being an outpost of the British Commonwealth . . . it's very difficult to have a complete cultural change in one generation. But, as an optimist, I believe that there are now companies, particularly large ones, which show that this can be done. And there are small ones who are picking up the theme.'

If an export culture is to permeate our manufacturing industry, many Australians who have never thought much about global trading, let alone experienced it, are going to have to start marketing their products overseas. It is not a facile step to be made by people following impatient whims. It involves careful planning and long-term commitment.

Potential exporters have to ask themselves a number of questions. Do they have good enough products which offer sufficient value to find niches overseas? Do they have the management and marketing expertise to sustain an overseas drive? Do they have the production capacity to develop and then sustain foreign markets? Or should they go into joint ventures or licensing arrangements? Do they have the financial strength to invest in the development of new markets before they see any substantial return?

Some manufacturers decide to ask and answer these questions independently. Others seek help and advice. That can extend to training: more than 40 Australian post-secondary institutions offer a wide range of courses which deal with export, ranging from a few days to full degree courses. Many exporters get assistance from official agencies, such as AUSTRADE. Others get it from private export specialists, industry organisations or even from overseas contacts.

This chapter looks primarily at some Australians who are starting out to export to one market—the United States—and at some of the people who are assisting them.

First, is John Chapman, a Sydney lawyer who has turned to marketing springs and suspension kits for off-road racing vehicles. He is making his own way into the US marketplace, but only after painstaking development of a product which is good enough for him to attract the support of a well-placed American joint venturer.

Next is an unusual married couple, Roger and Julie Bayliss. They are unusual because both work as trade commissioners in the AUSTRADE office in Los Angeles. Their work shows how Australian manufacturers can get a start in the US market with official help.

Finally there is a group of young people who undertake a special 'export marketing skills program' organised by the Centre for International Business at Monash University. Their course starts with lectures and desk-top market surveys in Melbourne. After that, they go to Los Angeles to study a potential market at first hand. This is not just an academic exercise; it is about survival in the real world. For all of this group are from the textile, clothing and footwear industry, which, with the lowering of tariffs, faces an uncertain future in Australia.

John Chapman loves off-road racing—with everything from special buggies and souped-up small sedans, fitted with impossibly large wheels, to light trucks and four-wheel drive vehicles bumping and sliding and flying through the dust or mud of bush tracks. He got caught up in it early by local standards, so much so, that he is known as the 'father' of off-road racing in Australia. But, before long, he realised that his greatest talents were not as a driver. He was, and is, an organiser: the kind of person who can put together a racing team and provide the support to help it win.

So he formed the 'Old Man Emu' racing team and developed special components, with the same name, for its vehicles. Sport and business merged and his hobby became part of his livelihood. He occasionally brought top drivers from overseas to help his team, 'names' such as Andrew Cowan, from Scotland, and American champion Rod Hall. And their association with his team helped him to sell his components.

The components he particularly specialises in are spring and suspension kits—essential for vehicles when drivers want to streak across pocked landscapes with the speed of cartoonist's roadrunner. He has the springs made in Sydney by National Springs, a BHP subsidiary, and the suspension gear in Adelaide by Monroe Australia. And he has proved them in the most rigorous Australian conditions.

Rod Hall, who has driven a lot of off-road vehicles in the United States, prefers them to American springs and suspension. He sees them as part of an Australian tradition of such componentry getting heavy usage in the Australian bush, 'the Outback'. Australian suspension 'has to work more than just look good,' he says. Americans, on the other hand, love to give their off-road vehicles a racy look by having their springs and suspension lift them way above the wheels. 'We're into lift kits,' he says, 'and, whether the ride like a buckboard, that's cool—we want them raised up.' It's a different tradition, stemming from soft, sloppy suspensions which can easily be unsafe when transferred off-road.

It was a growing friendship with Rod Hall which led to John Chapman deciding to try to sell his springs and suspension into the United States. Chapman describes Hall as 'the Peter Brock of four-wheeling' in the United States—a tribute to his mixture of driving, automotive and entrepreneurial skills. Hall, who has won all of the big off-road races in North America, remembers that Chapman phoned him from Australia in 1987 and told him he would like to get into the US market. Hall—'I'm a guy that kinda likes to do different things'—was intrigued. So he flew to Australia and, with Chapman, talked to National Springs and Monroe Australia. The result, says Hall: 'He and I formed an association and so we're going to do marketing of Australian suspension in the States.'

Hall brings to the association more than just the value of his endorsement as a champion driver. And the enthusiasm of the gung-ho racer does not overshadow his business sense. 'It's a very expensive hobby if you're not going to turn it in to some profit somewhere down the road,' he says. And he adds: 'Off-road racing in the States is big business today.'

Like Peter Brock in Australia, he has the status to be able to launch on to the US market personally endorsed, customised versions of standard vehicles. In his case, the vehicles are pick-up trucks. They are the pervasive vehicles of non-urban America and—in the same way that Range Rovers and their clones sprinkle Australian cities—of urban cowboys. And many of them are converted into off-road racers.

But before that stage was reached, Chapman and Hall had a lot of planning to do. One of the first decisions they made was not to use the 'Old Man Emu' name on componentry destined for the US. Americans, they discovered, generally did not know what an 'E-moo' was. So a new name was created: 'Australian Four-by-Four'.

Chapman knew enough about business and the experience of others before him to know his US foray would be difficult.

'It is a tough market to crack,' he says. 'I think a lot of people make the mistake of [thinking]—just because there's 240 million Americans—that it's going to be easy and they can snatch a couple of per cent of this market and that will do them. But it's not that easy. Of course, you have to have a reasonable "widget", as I like to refer to it, and there can be some problems in that. But, in reality, that's just where your problems are starting.

'I mean, you can go broke setting up your distribution costs and I've seen people make that mistake. And, even if you get your distribution set up without going broke, then your launch advertising costs are going to chew you. If you manage to solve your distribution, your launch advertising, your next problem's going to be that, God, they might even order the stuff, and now you've got to finance that bunch of stock. Now what happens if they re-order? Are your factories even going to be able to cope? So you've got to be very careful to proceed slowly and proceed certainly and be very realistic about what your up-front costs are going to be, before the dollars start rolling in on your selling.'

Rod Hall was especially important in helping solve two of those problems—distribution and launch advertising. First of all, Hall's name and contacts gave Chapman ready access to Dick Cepek Inc., America's biggest distributor of add-on parts for what the trade calls 'muscle machines'. If John Chapman was the father of off-road racing in Australia, Dick Cepek was the daddy of them all. He virtually invented it when he fitted wide wheels to ex-army jeeps and thus improved their ability to go into the unlikeliest places. The company he built on that basis is now run by his son, Tom Cepek.

So it was to Tom Cepek that Rod Hall took John Chapman in 1988 and a deal to distribute Australian Four-by-Four springs and suspension gear was made in the following year. In Los Angeles, Dick Cepek Inc. has an enormous warehouse which feeds parts to more than 6000 wholesale customers across the United States.

Rod Hall also helped get John Chapman into the Shelby Corporation in Los Angeles. The founder, Carol Shelby, built a huge business on his ability to make vehicles go faster. The company takes factory cars and pick-up trucks and, by changing engines and other key components, turns them into something more than the manufacturers intended.

In 1989, Chapman and Hall completed a deal with the Shelby Corporation to make and market a 'Rod Hall Special' using Australian Four-by-Four springs and suspension. Five hundred Dodge pick-ups will be given the treatment to turn them into top-of-the-line off-roaders. Chapman notes that the deal will give his products both distribution and exposure: 'That will be an add-on of $12 million worth of trucks with our gear running round.'

As for launch advertising, Chapman has taken some advertisements in specialist magazines. But this has been a minor activity. Rod Hall, in person, has been his best advertisement. In the last couple of years, Hall has driven in a number of major US off-road events with Australian Four-by-Four equipment. The events have included the Baja 1000 and the Baja 500, races which attract thousands of American enthusiasts to watch and compete as everything from buggies to trucks race across the desert of Baja California in north-west Mexico.

Chapman explains the purpose of competing for his company: 'We've done well in quite a number of major USA events—the problem being, of course, that no one's heard of good old Aussie BHP steel here. No one's heard of National springs. No one has really taken any notice of Aussie shocks. So we had to establish it.'

In the 1989 Baja 500, Hall drove a brand new vehicle and had to drop out because of engine trouble. But his team's number two truck came in second. And, most importantly, the Australian Four-by-Four parts on both trucks came through with flying colours. After the event, Chapman talked of the reaction he got: 'Do you see what they put steel through? I mean, no piece of steel is designed to go through what those guys do with it and, quite frankly, initially the race engineers here just did not believe me that we could produce stuff in good old Aussie that would last. Well, they've had to eat those words now because we did.'

Chapman is quick to point out that using major races as a form of advertising is not necessarily inexpensive 'because we're dealing with some very high-tech race trucks here'. But it is true, he says, that Australian Four-by-Four has been able to reach its distribution and launch advertising objectives 'by using our brains, rather than just having a giant, fat chequebook'.

The real profit for Australian Four-by-Four is in moving beyond the racing circuit and into the more general off-road market. And that is starting to happen, mainly through Dick Cepek Inc. and the Shelby Corporation. But there are other opportunities: the Los Angeles Country Sheriff's Department, for example, is now using Rod Hall Specials for off-road work. Hall is even giving tuition to some of the police. John Chapman hopes for more sales from it.

In his drive into the US market, Chapman has acted independently of official agencies. He had the advantage of legal skills and business acumen to help him go it alone. But it is not for the faint-hearted: 'I'm reasonably confident but, quite frankly, this market is a little daunting. You just can't think that, because you perceive yourself in your own market as being reasonably clever, you're going to be the same or regarded the same [in the US]. I think part of the mental problem—for me and maybe for Australians generally—is to get on top of this so you can feel comfortable in this marketplace, but without being too confident.'

Potential Australian exporters who are wary of trying to go it alone overseas have a ready-made alternative: using the services of AUSTRADE. AUSTRADE maintains offices in key locations throughout the world to advise Australian companies on export possibilities. Its services are available in a variety of ways, either on a cost-recovery basis or, in selected cases, through cost-sharing.

In a busy office, such as Los Angeles, staff will do at least some work on 20 to 30 individual products or product types every day. 'The variety is enormous—everything from gourmet foodstuffs to submersible tourist vessels,' says Roger Bayliss, a trade commissioner there. Under Senior Trade Commissioner Gerald Watkins, he works with another trade commissioner, three marketing managers and two research officers on the range of tasks.

Remarkably, the other trade commissioner is Julie Bayliss, his wife. They are the only married couple to work as trade commissioners in any AUSTRADE office. 'It's a considerable advantage,' says Julie Bayliss. 'It's not that we take work home every night but it's useful to have somebody who's doing the same job as you, whose opinions you trust, whose judgments you trust . . . We met in the job and we obviously have a high degree of compatibility. It's very useful: we work as a team.'

They moved to Los Angeles in 1987. Before then, they were in Baghdad, Iraq, where according to Roger Bayliss 'you might wake up to a missile explosion, where there's not much food in the shops, it's a war economy and you might have six or seven blackouts a day'.

Julie Bayliss tends to specialise in consumer products, while Roger Bayliss concentrates on industrial and technological goods. But, inevitably, there is overlap. And the aim is the same: to try to help Australian companies market their products on the US West Coast.

'The biggest assistance we can give a company is to get them into the market and kick-started,' says Roger Bayliss. A kick-start is to ensure that they're well informed about what they're coming into. This is a very affluent market; it's an excellent market for many of our companies that are starting off. But some of our companies make the mistake of thinking that, even though we speak the same language and because we enjoy a high degree of goodwill in this market, the American consumer will buy whatever it is we're selling and that, of course, is not the case.

'This is a highly competitive market. Point number one that I'd make is that many companies underestimate the intense competitiveness of this market. Being near enough is just not good enough. You have to really sharpen your prices, sharpen your performance and go for it in a very concentrated fashion, and not underestimate the complexities and costs of getting established.

'We can help companies get established. We can tailor program to suit their budgets in many cases. And, if they can't afford to dip their toes in the water, we're frank about telling them that. If, in fact, we believe that this is far too complex a market, we'll suggest others. It is a good market, though, and it can be segmented to find an area that is a good take-off point for smaller companies.'

On a fairly typical day in 1989, after talking to a visiting Australian manufacturer in his office, Roger Bayliss heads into suburban Los Angeles to check on the progress of a newly introduced Australian product. It is 'Kanga Ball' a set of plastic bat and stumps for a simplified form of cricket, so simplified that it would make even a colour-co-ordinated Kerry Packer player wince. The ball is bowled underarm— although the players call it 'pitching'—and the stumps, which are used without bails, are welded to a base so that they can be put in position on any surface.

Ironically, given its deviations from what would be acceptable at Lords or the Sydney Cricket Ground, it is being marketed overseas by the Australian Cricket Board. The board approached AUSTRADE to assess the general level of interest in such a game. Paul Erickson, a young AUSTRADE marketing specialist in Los Angeles, took it directly to primary schools and got a favourable reaction from teachers first and then children. So, in the land of baseball, Kanga Ball is now an approved sport in Los Angeles schools.

'If we go out and talk to the trade about games like this, they can say, "Well, yeah, maybe it's going to sell, maybe it's not",' says Roger Bayliss. 'We're in a position now to go direct to the trade and say, "Look, we've got a game, we know it's a performer, the kids like it".'

AUSTRADE has done the work for the ACB on a cost recovery basis. But Roger Bayliss's typical day also takes him to a Los Angeles boatyard to check on the progress of another Australian product which AUSTRADE is helping on a different basis. The product is the K & H range of polishes for pleasure boats.

In this case, AUSTRADE and K & H are sharing the cost for the preparation of a Company Export Plan (CEP) for the product. The CEP program is the latest means by which AUSTRADE tries to render its assistance most effectively. Its introduction followed a reconsideration of the traditional ways in which Australian trade commissioners had worked

The traditional way had been for trade commissioners to seek out trade opportunities and market intelligence and respond to exporters' enquiries. The trouble was that it found that the information-gathering service was not being used to maximum effect. The problems were varied. Enquiries too often related to markets where the relevant products had little or no chance of success. Companies were often not really ready to export because they lacked full commitment at the top, had done insufficient market-entry planning, had not prepared either their products or their production capacity to meet export needs, had not calculated costs and prices accurately, and so on.

AUSTRADE decided to introduce the CEP program in an effort to get its services to the exporters who can use them most effectively. It is managed by specialist trade commissioners in Sydney and Melbourne, who deal with companies throughout Australia. The ideal company is one which has successfully marketed its product in Australia to maximum potential and now wishes to get export business, or one which is already successfully exporting to one or more markets and wishes to expand into another region.

AUSTRADE applies the program in four stages. First an export proposal is reviewed by way of local desk-top research and an assessment of a company's capability. In the next stage, a market research brief is prepared, research is carried out overseas through AUSTRADE offices, the research is evaluated and a preliminary export report is drafted. By this stage, a good idea of potential overseas targets for a company and its products should have emerged. In the third stage, the company sends its own people overseas to validate earlier research, become familiar with the target markets and to meet recommended contacts; on return, they are debriefed. The final stage involves the preparation of an export plan. This includes analysis of the company, products and target markets; examination of strategic options; suggested programs and approach to target markets; resource requirements; preliminary forecasts; and future action plans.

The cost of the program to a company is between $5000 and $10 000, plus the costs of market visits. For its money, the company reduces the uncertainty of the export process:

its export manager will be familiar with the market, the appropriateness of the company's products, the competition, and the best way of getting orders. For its part, AUSTRADE applies its resources in the most cost-effective manner.

While Roger Bayliss is out giving K & H its money's worth, Julie Bayliss is on a different type of errand. She drives to Pasadena to finalise plans for a supermarket promotion of chilled lamb from Australia. The promotion is to be staged by Jurgensens, the leading gourmet supermarket chain in Los Angeles. In mounting the promotion, she is acting on behalf of the Australian Meat and Livestock Corporation which is hoping to export chilled lamb to the US West Coast for very high-income consumers. A highlight will be a series of barbecues at the store.

At the same time, the Australian producers of more than 30 other upmarket food and beverage lines have coat-tailed the promotion to achieve exposure for their products. Their products range from macadamia nuts to wine. Julie Bayliss is co-ordinating the endeavour, with the companies providing promotional support, some manpower and, of course, their products.

Julie Bayliss is quick to make the point that the marketing of food in the United States is so sophisticated that it is difficult to impossible for outside producers to compete in the market mainstream. But there are opportunities for processed food items at the top end of the market—'We are not competing with Kellogg's Corn Flakes,' she says—and for Australian wine.

She endorses her husband's comments on the difficulties of the US market: 'This is one of the toughest markets of all. The reason is that, when you export to this market it's not just a sales job; it's a marketing job. Frequently you're not selling a product on a [letter of credit], shipping the goods and seeing them go away over the horizon and that's that. In the States, you've often got to retain title to those goods right through to the store, right through to the point of sale. And that requires the involvement of the Australian exporter in every aspect of the distribution warehousing, the marketing and the retail process.

'Those who are first coming to this market need to lear

what is required of them, particularly as that impacts very considerably on the pricing of their goods.' The way in which the Australian exporter might have the ultimate responsibility for the movement of goods right through the market—even if dealing through a broker or distributor— is 'often the critical difference between the American market and others maybe a little less sophisticated than here'.

She cringes at the term 'flavour of the month' to describe Australian products. 'Certainly the Americans have a great empathy for Australia,' she says, 'and they're prepared to give an Australian product a second look. But it's a second look and then it must stand up on its own in being a distinctive product and keenly priced. If it doesn't have those competitive elements, as well as being from Australia, it's not going to do well, and it's a competitive product the market is looking for here; it's a distinctive product . . . The Australian product has to stand out, not just by being Australian but by being good.'

She sees a range of opportunities for Australian companies: 'If you've got a good product and you're prepared to get behind it, develop a good, solid marketing plan that's well capitalised; if that product is able to find a niche and create a demand, then it can certainly move into the US market. But it does require a commitment. The Australian company, the management of the exporting organisation, must really make a commitment to stand by their product—not just during that entry phase, which might be six months or a year, but . . . for maybe two or three years, till you get that effective pull-through effect so that the product develops acceptance in the market.'

In addition to the work of trade commissioners, AUSTRADE offers other services to exporters through its Australia-wide network of State offices. A key one is provided by AUSTRADE-EFIC, Australia's official export credit agency. It provides credit risk management services and specialist finance facilities for Australian exporters and investors overseas and their financiers.

'People moving into markets for the first time have the problem of selling more than just their product.' Slater Smith, AUSTRADE-EFIC's Group Development and

Services Manager, says. He explains how his organisation works by hypothesising a simple example of an Australian selling bananas to Taiwan: 'A banana is a banana. It may be no different from a Californian banana and [the Australian seller may] have to sell on better credit terms than the bananas coming from California. Being able to offer credit has its risks and, if you don't get paid, there is no export from Australia.

'What you have to think about as a new exporter is to consider protecting the payments coming back from Taiwan. And, just in the same way as you would insure your house or your car, you need to insure those payments that are receivable from overseas. You don't know the buyer in Taiwan. If you sell to someone in Woolloomooloo, you know where he lives; you can go and collect money in the evenings. If you're selling to someone in Taiwan or anywhere, you really need to have protection other than your own ability to collect money. So you take out an insurance policy, in the same way as you take an insurance policy for anything else. That's what we can provide.'

AUSTRADE-EFIC pays insurance claims worth about $8 million a year. 'We do more than just pay insurance claims though,' says Smith, 'because, if an exporter wants to cover his business with us, he has to tell us who his buyer is before we will decide whether or not it's worth our getting involved in it. And one of the most important things that we do is tell the exporter whether or not cover is available on a particular buyer. If we won't cover him, perhaps he shouldn't be exporting. So we save a lot of money before we even send our bananas to Taiwan.'

In April 1989, eight young executives from the textile, clothing and footwear (TCF) industries filed into a lecture room in Melbourne. They were there to begin to a crash course in export marketing skills. If they—and others like them—do not succeed in marketing their products overseas their very livelihood might be at risk. Because that is the dictum facing many of Australia's TCF industries: export or perish.

The Federal Government has introduced a TCF Indust

Plan, which involves a phased reduction of protection and a program to help manufacturers become more internationally competitive and to concentrate in areas of comparative advantage. For many, it will be a painful process as they become more exposed in the global marketplace. Yet people like Anne Lewin, whose activities are described in chapter 2, and Maggie Shepherd, from chapter 4, have shown that Australian designers and manufacturers can find good market niches overseas.

It was the hope of learning how to do just that that brought the young TCF executives to Melbourne from the five mainland states. They were attending just one of dozens of courses, dealing with export, which are now offered throughout Australia every year. Universities, TAFE colleges and organisations such as the Australian Institute of Export offer everything from brief introductory programs to full degree and diploma courses.

It is an area which, according to the practitioners, could do with greater co-ordination and, not surprisingly, more funds. They argue convincingly that one of our greatest export needs is for many more Australians to develop overseas marketing skills. Some people, such as John Chapman, of Australian Four-by-Four, might have the maturity and drive to teach themselves and go it alone. But a structured educational process would benefit most people starting out in the demanding world of export.

The TCF group had that benefit in 1989. They undertook a course run by Monash University's Centre for International Business and heavily subsidised by AUSTRADE and the Textile Clothing and Footwear Development Authority, which supervises the TCF Plan. It was broken into three phases. The first phase involved two intensive sessions, each of three days, in April and May in which they were given lectures and advice on exporting their company's products. Between these sessions, they carried out research into market opportunities. The second phase involved a two-week visit to the US West Coast in June to check out the possibilities there and to develop contacts and experience. The final phase was to draw structured export business plans for their companies.

The products represented by the young executives were as varied as their states of origin. They included fashion garments, bush hats, leather apparel, kitchen clothing, industrial fabrics and woollen jumpers. Some of the executives had had a taste of overseas marketing; some had not.

Take two of them as examples: Claudia Chan Shaw whose mother, Vivian Chan Shaw, produces upmarket knitted garments for women in Sydney; and Tim Grubi, from Queensland's Sunshine Coast, a former chef who has designed a new range of clothing for professional cooks and kitchen hands.

In 1980, when she was still in her teens, Claudia Chan Shaw went with her mother to North America to see if they could find a market for Vivian Chan Shaw's knitted garments. Their products are unusual: they take knitting out of the area of craft and into the world of fashion. And the Chan Shaws were unusual, as Vivian Chan Shaw recalls of that trip: 'It was a bit of a surprise to see a very young Claudia—because, at that stage, Claudia was still at college— and this strange Australian-Chinese, mad lady with a handmade line, an eccentric line, trying to sell to Americans.' Their main lesson from that trip: 'We learned that we knew nothing.'

But it did eventually lead to sales on the US East Coast. In 1987, Vivian Chan Shaw appointed an agent to look after marketing in New York. By 1989, it was time to explore the opportunities on the West Coast. That is where Claudia Chan Shaw's Monash course came in.

Tim Grubi's clothes are aimed for a much more workaday world. A New Zealander, he came to Australia to work as a chef and his occupation took him eventually to the Queensland resort town of Noosa. By the time he settled there, he had decided that the standard clothes for people working in kitchens could do with redesigning, particularly to make them easier to look after. Drawing on his observations of martial-arts clothing, track suits and jeans, he came up with clothes which made strong use of Velcro and studs. Dispensing with buttons made them easier to clean. And, by clever design, he created cooks' trousers a single size but with an adjustable pattern which enabled them to fit 80 per cent of people; for companies supplying clothes to employees, this was a boon.

Using a $50 sewing machine, he began to make the clothes for kitchen workers in Noosa in 1986. The following year, he turned it into a registered business. By 1989, he had long since given up cooking and was concentrating on his company, Chef Clothing Revival Pty Ltd. But he knew that in Australia he was looking at a finite market, so he wanted to expand overseas. That is what took him to the Monash course in Melbourne in April and May.

One of the lecturers was Melbourne businessman David Brown who had previously done a similar export course to help his company expand into the United States. He told the group one of the first lessons he had learned about the West Coast: 'If California was a country, it would be the seventh largest economy in the world . . . If Los Angeles alone was a country, it would rate the tenth biggest economy in the world. So Los Angeles alone has a bigger economy than Australia.'

That is an opportunity but also a challenge, as he explained: 'When you start looking at the American market and start putting together your plans for the American market, it is as well to consider that, if your product does take off, you can get very, very rapidly swamped in the American market because it is huge.'

Nigel Hamley, the course director, took Tim Grubi through some of the figures relevant to his product. Grubi had established that there are 4.2 million food service workers in the United States and, if they each bought three $100 uniforms a year, that would amount to an annual market worth about $1.3 billion. If the needs of bakers, pastrycooks and butchers were added to this, the total market would be worth about $1.8 billion. Hamley pushed the point home: 'If a market is that big, you really only need one per cent of it to have a viable business.'

Claudia Chan Shaw told Hamley how she had discovered through research that 5 per cent of American women spent more than $5000 a year on their clothing. They were to be her target. She also told the group of some good fortune:

two agents from Calmart, a large Los Angeles centre for clothing wholesalers, had walked into her mother's Sydney store unannounced and had liked the fashions; they had offered to arrange some meetings for her when the Monash group went to the US West Coast in June.

Before that trip, Tim Grubi broke away from the group to make a flying visit to Chicago for the US National Restaurant Association Exposition in May. He went purely to observe but got lucky: while there, he had a chance meeting with a wealthy American food processor who was looking to diversify his investment into related areas. There appeared to be a synergy between that ambition and Grubi's. So Grubi, too, had some meetings pre-arranged to coincide with the Monash group's US visit.

The West Coast meant a constant round of individual meetings with contacts for the Monash group. At the end of each day, they met back at their hotel to discuss their progress and the lessons learned, all under the eye of Nigel Hamley.

Claudia Chan Shaw was delighted to find that the experience was 'an absolute copybook for what Nigel said would happen'. She went on: 'He said, you've done your research; that's as much as you can do from Australia. You'll get to Los Angeles, you'll meet people, you'll start networking your contacts and somebody will refer you to somebody else and it's been exactly that way.' Without that course, she added, 'I wouldn't have researched as well as I did. It's all very well to do your door-knocking but you've got to know where you're going.'

Tim Grubi said the preparation for the trip 'opens your mind, it gets you understanding the variables, gets you questioning your own product. Once you can do that, I think you're on the right track.' The lesson of this for him: 'Don't leave Australia saying, "This is the product that I'm going to sell to the States", but saying, "This is the product that I've got to a stage which is acceptable to take to America to then redevelop for that market".'

By the end of the trip, Hamley was convinced that the members of the group would ultimately do well in the United States. 'I think we've got some unique products,' he said

'I think Australian design has got a lot to offer this market. The reaction that we've had . . . has really been most encouraging.' Of the immediate future: 'They're going to go back to Australia, do a lot more homework and then come back when they're ready with the right product, rightly priced, rightly packaged and with the sort of support— promotion, advertising programs—that will really make them successful here, rather than it being just a one-off selling trip.'

In fact, three months after the trip, Hamley predicted that the group would generate nearly $20 million worth of exports over the following year or two. That result would come from a Government investment of $50 000 in the course. Claudia Chan Shaw had received an order from a Los Angeles retailer. And Tim Grubi was about to sign a contract to extend his manufacturing into the United States in association with the food processor he had met at the Chicago exhibition.

The personal and company stories in this chapter have been about people exporting or trying to export Australian products to the United States. But they contain lessons which apply to other markets which Australia must penetrate more effectively. And, while the stories indicate that there are several ways of starting out in export, they have common elements.

Export needs commitment. It is not just a job for travelling salesmen. It requires strong direction and planning from the top. Export needs constant improvement of products to adapt them to market needs and to ensure that they offer top quality at a price which represents value. And that means knowing the marketplace—its opportunities and its pitfalls.

Finally, export is not for fly-by-night operators. It requires well-trained and motivated people settling in for the long haul to achieve long-term targets.

That all adds up to having an export culture. For too long, Australian manufacturing industry has not had one. Now, it must abandon the inward-looking habits of generations and get out into the world. It must go global. And it must do it now.